CAEN

The Brutal Battle and Break-out from Normandy

CAEN

The Brutal Battle and Break-out from Normandy

Henry Maule

BOOK CLUB EDITION

ISBN 0 7153 7283 1

This edition published by
Purnell Book Services Limited
P.O. Box 20, Abingdon, Oxfordshire OX14 4HE
by arrangement with David & Charles (Publishers) Limited.

Contents

1 Problem, Plan and Plot

General George Smith Patton Jnr, then the most hated commander in the US Army, made no attempt to disguise his angry impatience during the spring of 1944. He was eager to lead a crusading American army to shatter the Germans in France, not just because making war was in his blood but also because he had a bad name he must live down by achieving a notable victory. Additionally, Patton loathed General Sir Bernard Montgomery, the British commander-in-chief who was to direct the invasion. He had found Montgomery quite insufferable when their paths had first crossed in North Africa. He wanted to so out-general and out-dare this pompous, presumptuous Britisher that when the history of World War II came to be written the name of Patton would utterly dwarf that of Montgomery.

In fairness to Patton, he had been goaded. At one of the 'military critiques' the victor of El Alamein had given in the desert to both British and American commanders, he had declared that although American equipment was superb, their soldiers were so poorly trained and led that their equipment should be given to the British to get on with the war. In addition, Patton smarted at the knowledge that in their first clash with Rommel's Afrika Korps in Tunisia, the Americans had been trounced and had even run away. An American division, with the British 6 Armoured Division and a Guards brigade, had been ordered to force the Fondouk Gap to trap the Afrika Korps between the Anglo-American force and Montgomery's Eighth Army. When the attack went in the Americans complained of such severe casualties that they could not leave their foxholes. Lieut General John Crocker, the British commander of the operation, ordered a further attack. He acidly instructed

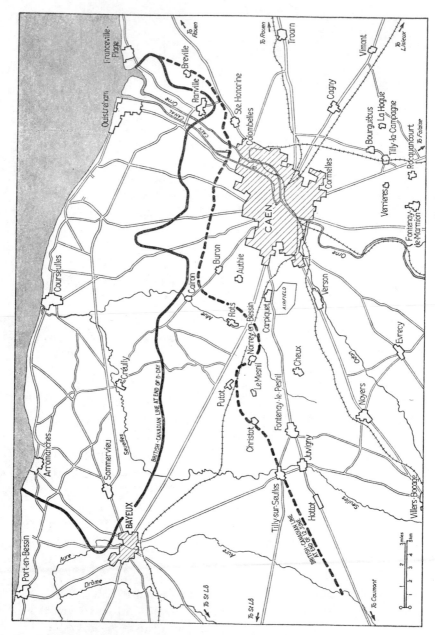

Map 1   The front before the first battle for Caen

a staff officer: 'Go and tell the American division's commander not to attack. I will do the job with a battalion of Guards.' The Fondouk Gap was duly forced and when General Omar Bradley arrived as General Eisenhower's representative Crocker told him that the reluctant American division's total casualties before taking to its foxholes were less than the casualties just one company of the Guards had suffered! This humiliation had continued to rankle in Patton's mind.

Until now Patton had only had one real opportunity of getting back at Montgomery, in Sicily. There his Americans, faced mostly by Italians, had raced across the western half while Montgomery's Eighth Army engaged in bitter fighting against the Germans up the other side. Patton had sworn he would be the first to reach Messina. He did, but en route took an opportunity of repaying the insult he felt Montgomery had inflicted on him and his men. He sent an officer with a five-gallon can of petrol to where Montgomery was temporarily halted at Taormina with the message: 'Although sadly short of gasoline myself, I know of your admiration for our equipment and can spare you this . . . It will be more than enough to take you as far as you will probably advance in the next two days.'

The bad name Patton had with American soldiers was the result of an incident in Sicily, which became a national scandal. He had slapped a shell-shocked GI in hospital and accused him of cowardice. Patton had nearly been cashiered. It was his fear now, as he waited in Britain, that the war in France would be over before he could get into it. Not only would he be denied his opportunity of showing Montgomery and the world how a war should be fought and won, but he would be remembered in American history only as 'the general who slapped a soldier'.

Although Patton had been given command of the American Third Army his immediate role was not to invade but to make the Germans *think* he would. He was required to show himself repeatedly near the south coast of Kent so that enemy intelligence could report his presence there. His spectacular advance in Sicily had stamped him as the Allies' most successful exponent of the armoured *blitzkrieg* and from his presence near the Straits of Dover the Germans were intended to deduce that the main invasion would be at the Pas de Calais, where the Canadians and British had already made an apparent reconnaissance in force with their bloodily repulsed Dieppe raid of 1942.

The deception plan was the brainchild of British Intelligence, to make the German High Command believe that the Normandy landings would be a diversion. For many weeks the RAF and USAAF had flown two reconnaissance missions over the Pas de Calais to every one over Normandy, and dropped twice as many bombs on the coastal defences across the straits as on those in Normandy. Similarly most of the bombing of the French railways was east of the Seine. To increase the deception, an elaborate combined operations HQ had been built at Dover and a pumping station for a cross-Channel petrol supply pipeline established there very obviously. New roads and railway sidings, camps, depots and concrete 'hards' for embarking tanks and transport from the beaches had been constructed there. Dummy landing craft were massed along the Thames estuary and dummy gliders littered airfields in Kent and East Anglia. German agents known to be operating in south-east England were allowed to observe all of this. Meanwhile enemy reconnaissance aircraft were permitted to photograph these dummy preparations.

A further distraction was organised in Scotland, where a fictitious Fourth Army appeared to be massing for the invasion of Norway, suggested by a mounting volume of wireless traffic. But the 'army headquarters' from which it emanated was no more than a skeleton HQ manned by Signals staff. German intelligence believed they had evidence of an intended landing in strength in Norway. As a result, German troops were kept very much on guard there.

The British deception plan was made even more convincing by the sending of all the radio signals from Montgomery's HQ just outside Portsmouth by landline to Kent to be transmitted. 'The formation of the Allied *schwerpunkt* [striking force] in southern and south-eastern England is again confirmed by the location of Montgomery's HQ', Field Marshal Erwin Rommel duly reported to the German Commander-in-Chief West

(Field Marshal Karl von Rundstedt). And von Rundstedt, whose achievements included the major role in the defeat of Poland, the break through to the Channel in 1940 and the spectacular advance to the Crimea and Rostov, who alone of the German commanders had never known defeat, was completely deceived. When he had planned the invasion of Britain in 1940, he had decided it must be where the Channel was at its most narrow. The massing of the American Third Army and the Canadian First Army opposite the Pas de Calais utterly convinced von Rundstedt, Rommel and Hitler—for once in complete agreement. The German High Command gave priority in reinforcements to the German Fifteenth Army north of the Seine. A formidable defence in depth was established behind the coastline between Le Havre and Calais.

The German High Command was determined that the Fifteenth Army should both block the short route to the vital Ruhr and protect the sites of the new V-weapons intended to terrify Britain into making peace. They massed 41 divisions in northern France and the Low Countries and 18 south of the Loire. The Fifteenth Army comprised 19 divisions while the Seventh Army had 10 divisions in Normandy. A further 56 divisions were on guard in southern Europe and 18 in Scandinavia. The Germans had 133 confronting the Allies and 165 against the Russians. Curiously, in view of the bitter lessons they had taught their adversaries about the power of massed armour, the panzer divisions in the west were scattered from Belgium to Bordeaux. The Allied air forces had won complete command of the air and smashed many of the factories that supplied the Luftwaffe. They had shattered road and rail routes which the Germans required to bring in forces for counter-attack. Many bridges over the Seine and most bridges across the Loire had been destroyed. Massive bombing of railway installations had created a 'railway desert' in northern France, especially behind the Pas de Calais.

The stage was set for Britain to send into battle a splendidly equipped and trained army nearly 1,750,000 strong, along with 175,000 Dominion forces and an American army and air force of 1,500,000 as well as some 44,000 from other nations.

The Allied air forces included 5,000 fighters and 4,000 bombers. The immediate object was to secure a bridge-head into Normandy from which massive military operations could be mounted. It had to contain port facilities to maintain a force of up to 30 divisions, to be reinforced by follow-up shipments direct from the United States as well as from Britain. In overall command during the invasion and establishment of the adequate lodgment area was Montgomery, under him the Twenty-first Army Group, consisting of the British Second Army with Canadian components and the American First Army. When the American Third Army was able to join the First Army they would be formed into the United States First Army Group under General Omar Bradley.

Montgomery's invasion plan envisaged the British capturing the medieval city of Caen, and the dominating heights beyond, *by the evening of D-Day*. To a maximum depth of 40 miles the countryside was mainly small fields bounded by stout hedge-topped banks, known as *bocage*. It was chequered with woodlands and orchards, criss-crossed with narrow, high-banked lanes and muddy-bottomed streams and studded with stout stone villages and farmsteads. It was ideal for defence, by anti-tank weapons and machine-guns in particular. To add to the difficulties for attackers the Normandy highlands ran, at a depth of up to 25 miles inland, from the south-east to the north-west, squarely across the invasion frontage. This was irregular broken terrain of abrupt hills and narrow valleys with its northern ridge dominated by the acutely steep scrub-covered Mont Pinçon, 18 miles south-west of Caen.

During the night before D-Day three airborne divisions, the British 6 and the American 82 and 101, were to be dropped behind the Germans' vaunted Atlantic Wall defences to secure the left and right flanks of the invasion bridge-head. The British were to establish themselves in the Orne valley on the left, the Americans were to form a line across the base of the Cotentin peninsula on the right. Soon after daybreak the main seaborne attack was to go in. The British Second Army, to land between Bayeux and Caen under the command of Lieut General Miles Dempsey, comprised XXX Corps on the right of the British sector, made up of the 50 Northumbrian Division and 8 Armoured Brigade, followed by the 7 Armoured Division and the 49 Infantry Division. The British I Corps in the left sector comprised the Canadian 3 Infantry Division and Canadian 2 Armoured Brigade, followed by Commandos of the 4 Special Service Brigade, the British 3 Infantry Division and 27 Armoured Brigade, followed by the 1 Special Service Brigade, the 51 Highland Division and the 4 Armoured Brigade. The American First Army, commanded by Bradley, to land north and east of the Vire estuary, comprised the US VIII Corps made up of the US 4 Infantry Division followed by the 90, 9 and 79 Divisions, and on their left US V Corps, comprising the US 1 Infantry Division with part of the 29 Infantry Division and the rest of 29 plus the 2 Infantry Division to follow up. The British-Canadian Force was to form a bridge-head between the rivers Vire and Orne, to include the towns of Isigny, Bayeux and Caen, while the Americans were to extend to the line of the Carentan Canal and onwards to the River Merderet.

Montgomery intended the British I Corps to seize Caen on the first day, with the open ground immediately south, while the British XXX Corps and American V Corps attacked southwards to capture the high ground along the line Cabourg–Villers-Bocage–Caumont–St Lô–La Haye-du-Puits. This was to be achieved by D + 9, by which time two 'Mulberry' artificial harbours would be in position to cope with the massive follow-up forces. It was considered the high ground of this line must be in Allied hands to prevent German artillery bombarding the harbours. Meanwhile, the British I Corps was to form a powerful bastion at Caen to withstand the anticipated main armoured onslaught of the inevitable German counter-attack and to provide a pivot for the all-out attack the reinforced Anglo-American armies would launch eastwards towards the Seine. The American VII Corps was to attack westwards, seal off the whole of the Cotentin peninsula, and secure Cherbourg to take over from the 'Mulberries'. Montgomery estimated this would be by D + 8, although Bradley thought D + 15. The Americans were then to launch an all-out attack southwards.

Montgomery estimated that by D + 50 (26 July) the Canadian First and American Third Armies would be in action and that the Americans would have captured the west coast Brittany ports, thence to pour in more divisions. He estimated that by D + 90 (4 September) the Allied armies would have advanced eastwards to the Seine and southwards to the line of the River Loire. Montgomery predicted Rommel would be too impulsive for a set-piece battle and would do his best immediately to 'Dunkirk' the invaders. He would not have the patience to concentrate to fight the decisive armoured battle on ground of his own choosing but would persist with counter-attacks in the *bocage* country, ideal defensive terrain full of death-traps for advancing armour and infantry. The Germans had made the most of it, filling it with well camouflaged defence posts and gun positions to a depth of six miles. Montgomery stressed that he would 'maintain a very firm left wing to bar the progress of enemy formations advancing from the eastwards'. In other words, the British and Canadians would take the full shock of the enemy armoured counter-attacks.

2 Omnipotent Panzers

On 9 June, three days after the Allied invasion force had poured ashore from near Ste Mere-Église in the west almost to France-ville-Plage in the east, a portentous conference took place in a field near the fishing village of Port-en-Bessin, attended by Generals Montgomery, Dempsey and Bradley. Jabbing at the map he had spread over the bonnet of his Humber staff car, Montgomery propounded his plan to simultaneously encircle the 21 Panzer Division and 12 SS Division, now defensively dug in around Caen. The British 3 Division, set to capture the city on D-Day, was still four miles short. The 51 (Highland) Division with the 4 Armoured Brigade would now execute a left hook out of the 6 Airborne Division's bridge-head east of the River Orne aimed at Cagny, six miles east of Caen, matched by a right hook from Bayeux towards Villers-Bocage, Noyers and Evrecy, led by the 7 Armoured Division (the 'Desert Rats'). When Cagny and Evrecy had been reached the British 1 Airborne Division would be dropped in between to complete Caen's encirclement.

An American attack was to drive forward parallel to the British armoured thrust, its objective Caumont. This however was to be only a diversion to disguise a major American effort to capture Cherbourg. The Allied attacks would soon be followed by a powerful Canadian advance on the left of the British thrust. The German command meanwhile believed that any apparent American threat to Cherbourg would only be a feint to distract them from a major British assault on Caen, itself a feint to draw the German Fifteenth Army away from the Pas de Calais. Meanwhile Montgomery's ultimate plan was that the British fought the maximum enemy strength between Villers-Bocage and Caen while the Americans thrust south and east to the Le Mans–Alençon area and beyond. The enemy

15

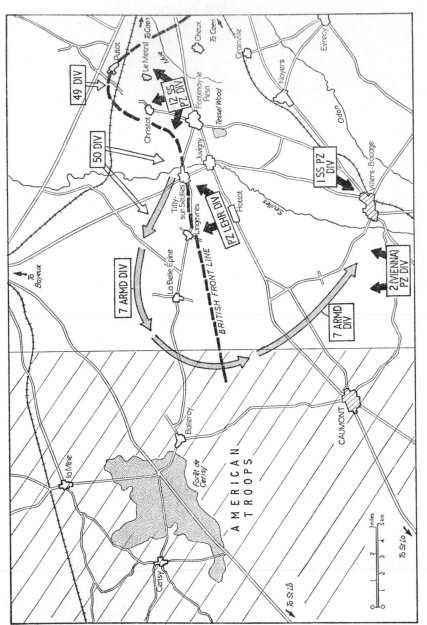

Map 2　Right hook for Villers-Bocage 12–15 June

Plate 1. With his campaign map before them on the bonnet of his staff car, General Montgomery seems to be in genial agreement with Generals Dempsey and Omar Bradley on his plan for the Anglo-American assault out of the Normandy bridgehead

Plate 2. British soldiers with a 17-pdr anti-tank gun look at a German Panther tank just knocked out. They are on a Bren carrier with which they both tow their gun and themselves ride into action. The 17-pdr was one of the few British guns capable of stopping the heavy German Panther and Tiger tanks

Plate 3. Tanks of the 7th Armoured Division (the 'Desert Rats') were briefly able to embark on a really mobile attack at Villers Bocage – 'Going swanning' they had called it in their desert days. But in Normandy their apparent breakthrough was blasted back by massive enemy counter attack

would be forced back against the Seine with no way of escape.

The Allied and German commands were unwittingly planning simultaneous onslaughts. The Germans intended to drive the British and Canadian invaders right back into the sea. The British bridge-head was seen as the more dangerous because the Germans had a low regard for the Americans as fighting men. Now General Geyr von Schweppenburg, commanding the Panzer Group West, and General Kurt Meyer, commanding the 12 SS Panzer Division, planned to advance to the coast with three armoured divisions. Meyer was confident that his troops, the pride of the Hitler Youth, would hurl the British back into the sea. He described them as 'little fish'.

The British were suffering from delays in the landing of follow-up divisions and unloading of ammunition, caused by bad weather. The 21 Panzers were ordered to advance on the right from Caen, the Panzer Lehr Division on the left from near Bayeux, with the 12 SS Division between them. It was to be an all-out effort to defeat the Allies while they were still in their beach-head. Inevitably the violent British and German assaults must meet head-on.

The Germans struck first, on 10 June. An armoured battle group supported by an infantry division attacked the 6 Airborne Division's bridge-head and gained some ground before being halted with disastrous losses. The unco-ordinated drawing of the Highland division in to the battle to strengthen threatened points prejudiced their divisional attack. Infantry losses on both sides were particularly severe and the fighting became very bitter after the Scots discovered the Germans had shot prisoners. Hand-to-hand fighting of the utmost savagery, in which the Black Watch was heavily involved, lasted almost non-stop for three days and nights. But what finally established the unchallenged British hold on their Orne bridge-head was an heroic night attack by 160 Paratroopers at Breville. At the cost of 141 casualties they annihilated a German battalion. When the Scots finally made a brigade attack they collided head on with the formidable Battle Group Luck and both attacks shuddered to a bloody halt.

The western German threat saw tanks of the Panzer Lehr

B

Division meet armour of the British XXX Corps. On the centre
sector, meanwhile, the Canadian 3 Infantry Division set off in
high spirits on a perfect summer's day, the infantry riding on
the tanks of the Canadian 6 Armoured Regiment. Suddenly
among German panzer grenadiers hidden in rippling cornfields
they dropped off to give battle. The tanks rolled on until, as
they topped a gentle rise, they were subjected to devastating
enemy artillery fire. They drove on to Le Mesnil Patry and
advancing further they found German tanks and anti-tank guns
awaiting them at St Mauvieu on their left front and Christot on
their right. Realising the danger of his small force being surrounded the regimental commander ordered them back to the
Caen road. The Canadian tanks had suffered heavily. Everywhere along the line of their advance were burning tanks,
billowing black smoke from the midst of cornfields, orchards
and hedgerows. The Canadian 6 Armoured had lost 37 tanks
and in the leading company alone the infantry had sustained
close on 100 casualties.

Canadian infantry and tanks were hurried forward to dig in
between Bray and Rots to confront an expected counter-attack
by the 12 SS aimed at reaching the coast. At dusk a force of the
crack 46 Royal Marine Commandos stormed into Rots and
fought savagely hand to hand with Hitler Youth storm troopers
of the Waffen SS. Casualties were high on both sides. The day's
fighting had been of brutal ferocity, and many stories now
circulated that Kurt Meyer's SS division were executing
prisoners. As a result an Order of the Day was published that
prisoners would not be taken. James McDonald of Cornwall,
Ontario, a corporal in the Stormont, Dundee and Glengarry
Highlanders (The Glengarries), recalls his company sending
out a reconnaissance patrol on which Lieut Fred Williams and
Private Pollard were wounded, taken prisoner and shot on the
orders of Meyer. Irrefutable proof of Meyer's savagery is given
by Dr Donald Isaac of Port Talbot, then a British Army MO.
He remembers: 'Kurt Meyer shot 25 Canadians and 1 Durham
Light Infantry major in a chateau outside Caen because they
"would not talk". I performed the post mortem examinations
with a Canadian pathologist.'

Many of the British and Canadian troops, particularly the latter, now went into battle fighting mad. But on both sides the troops were fought to a standstill so that both the German offensive towards the sea and the British and Canadian drives to encircle Caen shuddered to a halt. The battlefield was littered with burned-out tanks, and fields of ripening corn were scorched and strewn with the blackening corpses of both sides.

The only appreciable penetration by the British offensive was on the right flank where the 7 Armoured and 50 (Northumbrian) Divisions, strengthened by some independent tank and infantry brigades, advanced from the west towards the strategic Villers-Bocage ridge. In their path stood the crack Panzer Lehr division commanded by General Fritz Bayerlein, Rommel's chief-of-staff in North Africa, armed with the heavy Panther and Tiger tanks. 7 Armoured had only the new Cromwell tanks, light and fast and intended for mobile warfare. Now they were required to challenge much heavier and more heavily armoured panzers which outgunned them under conditions which prevented fast manœuvre. The German Panther weighed 45 tons and was armed with a long-barrelled 75mm gun. The Tiger, weighing 56 tons, had an 88mm gun, and the Royal Tiger weighed 67 tons and was armed with an even more powerful 88mm gun. By comparison the heaviest Allied tank was the British Churchill, just under 40 tons, while the Sherman, with which the majority of Allied armoured units were equipped, weighed only 30 tons. And whereas the enemy high-velocity guns could penetrate the Allied tanks, the shells from most Allied guns, more especially from their tank guns, just bounced off the thick armour of the Tigers and the Panthers.

The confusing Normandy *bocage* gave the German tanks full scope to dig down out of sight, ready to pick off the advancing British. Also hidden among the hedgerows were infantry with anti-tank guns and sticky bombs, as well as many devastating 88mm guns. In such unfavourable conditions, and without close infantry support, the Desert Rats were unable to make appreciable progress. Fierce enemy counter-attacks with armour were only beaten off after savage night fighting. The 50 Division meanwhile had been heavily engaged fighting on either flank of 7 Armoured. The Green Howards and Dragoon Guards had attacked towards Christot, successive waves of tanks and infantry plunging forward among the hedgerows, deep ditches and sunken roads. The bitter close-quarters fighting produced heavy casualties. Positions captured on high ground at Point 103 were held after savage fighting.

Ranging over this confused and bloody battlefield, the Allied fighters, bombers and fighter-bombers were very effective. At the Battle HQ of Panzer Group West only General Geyr von Schweppenburg survived, his chief-of-staff and 17 staff officers all being killed. With them were buried Rommel's immediate hopes of a decisive counter-attack. Sepp Dietrich, commanding the I SS Panzer Corps, who now took over from von Schweppenburg, at once scrapped the counter-attack plan because he believed the British were about to make an all-out assault on Caen. Although the British and Canadians. had failed to attain their immediate objectives, they were nevertheless bloodily fulfilling Montgomery's requirement to attract the mass of the enemy armour against them. 'By the evening of June 12 we had celebrated our first week ashore without a single threatening counter-attack on the American beach-head,' Bradley was able to note. And indeed the Americans were reporting 'no real opposition' as they advanced steadily upon Caumont, 20 miles inland. Rommel had ordered that any American penetrations must be sealed off by infantry divisions already on the spot.

The American V Corps had made some remarkable progress. Daring night marches by the 29 Division had opened the road through Isigny and outflanked the German defences there. And when Montgomery ordered Bradley to exploit rapidly southwards towards St Lô and Caumont, he could do so immediately. By the evening of 11 June the American 2 and 1 Divisions were 14 miles south of their beach-head and level with the British. Meanwhile the only fresh troops the Germans had been able to send against them were two battalions of cyclists and six assault guns! The obvious ease of the American advance persuaded Montgomery to move his main attack on Caen further westwards where a system of minor roads and tracks seemed to provide suitable terrain for a thrust to out-flank Panzer Lehr. The strategic ridge beyond Villers-Bocage, the original objective, could still be attacked.

The British XXX Corps had by 12 June fought forward to a line La Belle Epine–Lingevres—Tilly–Fontenay-le-Pesnel–Christot–Bronay, all village fortresses linked into a system of anti-tank defences backed by armour and heavily armed infantry. Montgomery decided to launch 7 Armoured into a sweeping attack from the west, to thrust on towards Evrecy and the high ground between the Odon and the Orne. When 7 Armoured were stealthily extricated from the suicidal *bocage* country many imagined that once more there would be a chance to exploit their manoeuvrability. Leaving the tough Northumbrian infantry locked in battle with Panzer Lehr, they drove through the American sector and a gap in the German defences to come in behind the German armour at Villers-Bocage.

Colin Thomson, from Manchester, an armoured car driver-operator in the 11 Hussars, recalls:

'My troop penetrated . . . as far as Cahagnes where . . . we saw a large concentration of enemy armour moving towards Villers-Bocage. Round the corner of a narrow lane came a German 8-wheel armoured car. Its commander descended and began to walk down the lane towards our officer's vehicle obviously believing we were Germans. It wasn't until he came within 100 yards that his suspicions were aroused. He dropped his binoculars and bolted into the thick hedge. Our lead car gunner let go. The Jerry vehicle went up in a cloud of smoke.

'We heard another vehicle which appeared to be retreating. The realisation that the German vehicle might be moving round to cut us off prompted speedy retreat. Within five minutes a heavy rumble denoted the approach of a vehicle and all our guns were trained on to the lane down which it was coming. The tension grew as the roar and rattle increased. "Please God it's not a Tiger!" someone said. It turned out to be a huge self-propelled gun which we hit with everything we had, destroying it and its crew.'

On the morning of 13 June tanks of the 4 County of London Yeomanry with infantry of the Rifle Brigade riding in half-tracks, entered Villers-Bocage without opposition. There, 6 miles behind the enemy lines, they stormed on through the town heading for the vital high ground of Hill 213 that dominated the National Highway where it thrust straight to Caen. A way seemed to have been found to Montgomery's declared main D-Day objective. A closely packed little armoured column of Cromwell and Honey light tanks, half-tracks and carriers rattled triumphantly towards the vital hill-top. But behind the crest lay in wait components of the 501 Heavy SS Tank Battalion with four Tigers and a strong force of infantry. The Tigers' commander, Obersturmfuhrer Wittman, was a tank ace from the Russian front with the formidable record of 119 enemy tanks destroyed. He now opened up on the half-track leading the British onrush and the high-velocity projectile from his huge 88mm gun left it shattered and blazing across the road, blocking it. The great Tiger then ground forward along the line of the British vehicles picking them off. One after the other they disintegrated while the shells from the British tank guns bounced off the Tiger's immensely thick armour. The rest of Wittman's Tigers surged out to complete the annihilation of the daring Desert Rats' spearhead. The British losses included 25 tanks, 14 armoured trucks and 14 Bren carriers.

But when the apparently omnipotent panzers rumbled on into Villers-Bocage, they were confronted by British infantry of the Queen's Regiment. One after another the Tigers became fiery death traps as British soldiers stalked them and from close quarters blasted them in known weak spots with Piat projectiles.

'By the time we reached the outskirts reports spoke of extremely hard fighting there,' Colin Thomson remembers. 'We began to work up north and north-west and also to the south where, at Tracy-Bocage, the troops came under heavy fire from 88mms. Heavy machine-gun fire started up along our southern flank and the Colonel decided to send all "soft" vehicles to the rear. It became clearer by the minute that we were in for some trouble in keeping our centre line intact. Meanwhile the 4 CLY and the RBs were taking some stick in Villers and beyond. German tanks had managed to get behind them and cut up their RHQ while further on a whole squadron was "treed" on top of a hill by Tigers sitting round the bottom. Of this party only a few managed to get out.'

But the exciting British thrust behind the enemy was doomed. Yet another German panzer division, the 2 Vienna, had arrived, before the expected reinforcements of British armour and infantry (two days late because of rough seas) meant to exploit the penetration by 7 Armoured. It was decided to pull back the under-gunned tanks of the Desert Rats, which were too light to face the 2 Vienna Panzer Division and Panzer Lehr. In Africa they had already learned the lethal qualities of the 88mm guns, which could destroy them while they were still far outranged. (In fact, when veteran Desert Rats played 'Housey' the caller never said '88—all the eights' but '88—driver reverse'.) In addition, the snipers' paradise *bocage* country was suicide to tank commanders accustomed to fighting with heads out of open turrets.

Cyril Cadman of Lower Gornal, near Dudley, then a L/Bdr driver with the 15 Medium Regt, RA, remembers one night before this attack sharing a dug out with a sergeant of the Desert Rats. When told of the bitter fighting which had already taken place over the terrain around, he declared it would not take *them* long to shift the bloody Germans. 'After the bombs and shells dropped on the German positions it was hard to believe they could stand the carnage,' recalls Cadman. 'The smell was impossible to describe. Not only did the Germans stand all this, but they fought back and gave the Desert Rats the biggest shock of all.'

On 14 June, powerful enemy armoured forces converged from three sides upon the defensive box, some 1,000 yards by 700 yards, into which 7 Armoured had formed themselves. Fighting was desperate before the German panzer grenadiers were finally blasted back by 7 Armoured's attendant artillery firing point-blank over open sights.

'The Germans mounted a heavy attack and we were all lined up to take them on if they should penetrate our area,' remembers Thomson. 'The 3 and 5 RHA were firing over open sights into the woods 300 yards away through which the enemy were advancing. We were also getting help from a large number of medium guns turned on by the Americans at Caumont. The result was unbelievable carnage. This battle lasted until 10.30pm when Jerry decided to retire and presumably regroup.'

Ultimately, covered by an Allied artillery barrage and an RAF night bombing attack, the British division was pulled back 7 miles. Its new line extended from just west of Villers-Bocage to ground held by the US 1 Infantry Division near Caumont. It was the Desert Rats' first taste of defeat since El Alamein, a bitter experience even though they had caused the destruction of dozens of enemy tanks and large numbers of their infantry. They were now to await the arrival of an additional armoured brigade, delayed in landing, before attacking again. Had this brigade with its 150 tanks and an infantry brigade arrived on schedule, the Villers-Bocage right hook might well have succeeded.

There were now four German armoured divisions facing the British, and Montgomery decided to go on to the defensive before Caen and to exert pressure around Caumont. He had ordered Bradley to hold Caumont firmly while the Americans cut off the Cotentin peninsula and took Cherbourg. Montgomery's immediate objectives were Caen and Cherbourg and the expanding of the bridge-head's central sector to Caumont and Villers-Bocage. The US V Corps had widened its salient towards the British sector by pushing through the Forêt de Cerisy and penetrating the outskirts of Caumont even as the British 7 Armoured Division had attacked. Meanwhile the American VII Corps had taken Carentan, the German garrison having expended all their ammunition. Omar Bradley now ordered up his XIX Corps to attack towards St Lô.

3 The Fatal *Bocage*

As the British and the Americans consolidated, von Rundstedt urgently appealed for reinforcements. He had already committed three additional armoured divisions and two infantry divisions to contest the British advance, which he took to be the main danger. But he had been unable to concentrate his panzer divisions to smash through the Allied bridge-head. Hitler's reaction was to order II SS Panzer Corps (the 7 and 10 SS Panzer Divisions) from the Russian front 'to annihilate the British bridge-head'. There could be no question of retiring to a new line. 'Every man shall fight and die where he stands', decreed their Fuhrer, from his bomb-proof bunker so many hundreds of miles away.

Montgomery had hardly switched his attack to Caumont before the 2 Panzer Division pushed in that direction and the main battle moved there. 'So long as Rommel uses his strategic reserves to plug holes that is good,' Montgomery reported to Eisenhower. The battle now was entirely in the mazy *bocage* country at close quarters, in which the Germans were initially superior. Their experience fighting in Russia had fitted them much better for the *bocage* battle than the British soldiers' experience of mobile warfare in the wide wastes of the North African desert. The Germans had the additional motive that unless they triumphed the Allies would surely carry devastating warfare into Germany.

The massed British and American artillery heavily bombarded the advancing 2 Panzers. It seemed that everywhere the earth was erupting, and steel splinters rent the air. To these veterans of the Russian front it was a bombardment of unparalleled fury. It caused many to believe that the manually loaded 25 pounders of the Royal Artillery were power operated.

When it ceased the ensuing silence was broken by a swarm of RAF rocket-firing Typhoons sweeping out from the morning mist. At tree-top height they plunged in to the battle, streaking rockets into dug-in enemy positions and half-hidden vehicles and raking them with cannon and machine-gun fire. As the Typhoons wheeled away, the smouldering battlefield was ghastly with the screams of mortally wounded men and the bellowing of mutilated farm animals. It was already widely strewn with the stinking corpses of farm animals, grotesquely bloated and crawling with maggots. Among the more horrible experiences of the soldiers dug down in foxholes was to have the putrifying corpse of a cow blown by an erupting shell across the hole.

Despite the very heavy bombardments ('Pandemonium' was the code word for a full-scale American contribution) the 2 Panzers took Launay and St Germain d'Ectot on their right on 17 June, suffering dreadful losses. On the left an attack which reached le Quesnay suffered heavily when counter-attacked by British tanks and infantry. Desperate house-to-house fighting ensued and after ground captured by the enemy had been subjected to an obliterating creeping barrage, the Germans were pushed back. The 2 Panzers returned to the attack on 18 June and pushed through to Briquessard, but at fearful cost. This veteran armoured division—which had tasted heady victory in Poland, at the Maginot Line, at Boulogne in 1940, against the New Zealanders in Greece, and in great tank battles in Russia to the very suburbs of Moscow—was being decimated in Normandy. Although the British had also suffered heavily they were achieving precisely what Montgomery intended—the annihilation of the German armour. He meanwhile reiterated that his general policy remained 'to pull the Germans on to the British Second Army and fight them there so that the US First Army can carry out its task easier'.

The life of an infantryman, on both sides, was often short. With two armies of such fire-power locked so furiously in such close combat, mere flesh and blood stood little chance. Death or maiming was almost inevitable. In addition the big guns of rampaging tanks blasted the foot-soldiers at close quarters, depressing to fire high-velocity shells in to trenches and foxholes to commit hideous butchery. In the closely hedged and ditched *bocage* country it was often impossible during a lull to observe a single fighting man or machine. But the clouds of flies, the smoke acrid from charred flesh lazily streaming on the soft summer breezes, and everywhere the hasty grave mounds topped with crude wooden crosses, or with boltless rifles or steel helmets, indicated where enemies had succeeded in achieving the purpose for which they came into this verdant Normandy countryside.

The leading armoured car of a patrol, often with commanding officers and crew, was frequently destroyed by enemy 88s, easily camouflaged in the thick hedgerows bordering the narrow winding lanes. This happened so frequently that the order of march was altered to conserve the officer material. The second car, commanded by the Troop Sergeant, took over the lead position. Patrols were usually in enemy territory, creeping down narrow overgrown byeways with possible destruction waiting round every turn. To carry on like this, day after day, became intolerable and the troops relied heavily on alcohol to induce a feeling of confidence and relaxation. Often they drank calvados, diluted with red wine or rough cider, which they called 'Stupor Juice'. Most armoured-car crews had a bottle with them each time they went out on patrol.

With all the squandering of life and machines, speed of reinforcement was obviously the key to the battle. The Germans had to reinforce overland faster than the Allies could across the sea. And in this the dominating Allied air-power dictated the course of events. The Anglo-American reinforcements flowed across uninterrupted, while the Germans moved theirs overland at their constant peril. The planes of the RAF and USAAF bombed and rocketed troop trains and transport columns 30 miles and more from the battle front. One SS division despatched soon after D-Day disintegrated beneath the fury of Allied air attacks and its scattered formations skulked in woods until night. It was almost impossible for Rommel to bring in fresh divisions as battle-ready formations. They had to make their way to the front by night in scattered units, often on foot or by bicycle. Much of their armour and heavy fighting equipment was destroyed *en route*. So far and wide did Allied aircraft range that the two SS panzer divisions switched from the Russian front were in trouble long before they reached Normandy. The first took longer to cross the last 400 miles than it had taken over all the 1,300 miles from Russia to the French borders.

In addition the enemy were shaken by the immensity and accuracy of the Naval bombardments. This shelling, directed upon them by OP officers in spotter planes, was carried out by a variety of warships, including battleships capable of obliterating targets 16 miles inland around Caen. During the night of 12/13 June, for example, the battleships *Nelson* and *Ramillies* sent a 15in shell into Caen every 30 seconds! This was particularly heartening to the British and Canadian infantry crouching in their slit trenches. They would see the sky behind them glare with the flash of the great guns, hear the ripple of the huge projectiles rushing over them, then listen for the explosions in enemy territory.

Hitler now launched the full force of his ultimate V-weapons against the British people. The V1 flying bombs began to explode indiscriminately on London and across south-east England, launched from the Pas de Calais where the German Fifteenth Army was still held in readiness. Hitler was convinced his new terror weapon would either make the British people scream for mercy and their government sue for peace, or would so enrage them that Patton's army would be rushed across the narrow straits to its inevitable doom. That must be the end of the war in the west with the Normandy invaders scuttling back as fast as they could go. Then all German forces would be available to hurl against the Russians and end the war in the east as well. In fact the British decided to 'grin and bear it' as they had during the Blitz of 1940–1. On 18 June Winston Churchill impressed upon Eisenhower that there must be no change of plans aimed at making an early conquest of the territory containing the V1 launching sites. London and the south-east of England would endure the bombardment for just as long as was necessary. But for two months Bomber Command diverted half of its efforts to attacking V1 installations, which directly contributed to the Allied deception that the main invasion had still to come across the Straits of Dover. Rommel reported to von Rundstedt on 19 June: 'A large-scale landing is to be expected on the Channel front on both sides of Cap Gris Nez or between the Somme and Le Havre. This fresh landing may be timed to coincide with the general offensive from the Normandy bridgehead.'

Haunted by the grim spectre of a main Allied invasion still to come, Rommel dared not switch the infantry divisions from the Fifteenth Army so desperately needed to engage the British and Canadians and release the mass of his panzers against the 'soft' Americans. They had made such dramatic progress in the Cotentin peninsula with virtually no armour against them that they had driven a line right across it to the west coast at Barneville. There had been a significant regrouping of the American forces and on 15 June the US VIII Corps became operational with the 90 Infantry Division and both American airborne divisions under command. They were to protect the rear of the imminent attack to capture Cherbourg. Meanwhile the US XIX Corps fought southwards towards St Lô. By 18 June the US VII Corps was facing north with three divisions from Barneville to Caumont, while facing south along this line were the US VII, XIX and V Corps. Flooded low-lying terrain and marshes were preventing their further deployment.

Rommel now had two main tasks, to contain the bridge-head and to gather together an armoured force powerful enough to steamroller them back into the sea. Although so far he seemed to be achieving the former it was at the undoubted expense of the latter, because he was having to squander his armour plugging gaps forced by the British attacks. Meanwhile, compelled to look to Holland and the south of France for further infantry reinforcements, he was aware that the Allied aircraft would delay their arrival and made it doubtful, unless there was really bad weather, that he would ever be able to risk massing his panzers. As Montgomery continued to mount attacks which were bloody and costly to his own and enemy troops, he was forcing Rommel to use his tanks as dug-down artillery instead of massing them for the coming offensive.

On the American front progress was slow and steady. They had entered Carentan after some hard fighting, and had surged forward to Caumont. Their spectacular thrust across the Cotentin peninsula had isolated the vital port of Cherbourg. The inspiration had been Lieut General J. (Joe) Collins, who had already in 1943 achieved fame commanding an infantry division against the Japanese on the island of Guadalcanal, where they had defeated the Japs in a series of savage engagements through thick and swampy jungle. After Guadalcanal Collins found the Cotentin *bocage* relatively easy. He leapfrogged the experienced US 9 Division into a series of short, sharp thrusts utilising maximum infantry fire-power on narrow fronts and penetrating to the west coast. He had been able to risk ignoring his flanks because of the enemy's lack of any armour. Meanwhile Hitler's obsession that there should be no retreating had virtually doomed the German force on the Cotentin peninsula. He forbade their withdrawal into Cherbourg's strong perimeter fortifications. Collins regrouped his force and struck fast and hard northwards for Cherbourg. Before nightfall they had broken the main German position, throwing them into confusion. Only twenty-four hours later Collins had three divisions poised on the very threshold of Cherbourg; the bulk of the troops who should have been defending this formidable fortress being caught still outside. Inside were no more than 21,000 men, comprising the remnants of four battered divisions, labour corps men and various naval personnel, marine gunners and anti-aircraft gun crews. 'The fighting ability can only be described as inferior,' reported Lieut General Karl von Schlieben, the battle group commander on the Cotentin. He complained that a fifth of his force were foreigners and 'you can't expect Russians and Poles to fight for Germany against Americans in France'. Short of ammunition and supplies, the garrison finally gave in on 26 June.

By comparison with the Americans' progress the story on the British front continued to be the bloody non-stop slogging, holding down the German armour at the expense of British and Canadian lives. It was significant at this time that King George VI landed in Normandy (Churchill had done so on 10 June) openly to visit the British and Canadian troops. The next day when Hitler arrived in France for a conference near Soissons it was at a fortified command post built in 1940 from which he had intended to conduct the invasion of Britain. Both Rommel and von Rundstedt indicated to Hitler that they wanted to withdraw to fight from the line of the Seine, a battle in which they could use armoured divisions as they were meant to be used. Sepp Dietrich had complained to Rommel: 'I am being bled white and am getting nowhere.' The Allies now had 20 divisions, a total of some 557,000 men (279,000 British, 278,000 American) ashore in Normandy, having achieved a much faster build-up than the Germans, who had 18 divisions, many badly mauled. Rommel and von Rundstedt even ventured to suggest that Hitler should sue for peace. Angered, the Fuhrer seemed obsessed with a conviction that his new V-weapons would win the war. With nothing resolved he flew to his mountain refuge at Berchtesgaden.

Two days later the elements intervened to the Germans' advantage. The worst June gale for nearly half a century raged through the Channel from 19 June for three days and nights. It drove 800 vessels ashore, sank dozens out at sea, wrecked most of the 'Mulberry' artificial harbour off the American beach-head, and severely damaged the 'Mulberry' off Arromanches. The sudden grave curtailment of supplies, particularly of ammunition (against 24,412 tons landed on the 18th, there were only 4,560 tons on the 20th) forced Montgomery to postpone an imminent attack. Dietrich had warned Rommel that if replacements did not come soon the front could not be held in the event of an attack. The very fact that Rommel was unable to mount a counter-attack at this moment showed how the brutal war of attrition on the British sector had squandered his panzers. However, because the Americans now only had enough ammunition for three days, Bradley had to postpone his planned break-out which meant the British and Canadians had to go on fighting the major enemy strength for days longer than contemplated. And because the gale had prevented three British divisions being landed they had to do so with far fewer troops than expected.

Montgomery had planned a major offensive, to take Caen by envelopment, to begin on 22 June. But it had to be postponed until the 25th. The Americans, meanwhile, had been repulsed in a determined attempt to take St Lô. Bradley was not satisfied with the co-operation between his tanks and infantry. There were in England 15 divisions awaiting shipment to Normandy and the British Army had 6 training divisions supplying reinforcements. Yet so effective was the British deception plan that German Intelligence was even now reporting that 'in England another 67 major formations are standing to, of which 57 at the very least can be employed for a large-scale operation.' At such an ominous time as the fall of Cherbourg, the Germans were still keeping more divisions on guard at the Pas de Calais than committed to the Normandy battle. On 26 June Rommel warned von Rundstedt of an imminent 'large-scale landing between the Somme and Le Havre'.

Plate 4. A German dual-purpose anti-aircraft/anti-tank 88mm gun, which dominated the Normandy battlefield. So high was its muzzle velocity, lethal to every type of British and American tank, that its heavy projectile arrived well before the roar of the gun was heard

Plate 5. British 25-pdr guns bombard a German counter-attack. The British gunners kept up such a rapid rate of fire that the Germans were convinced these guns must be power operated

Plate 6. In the close bocage country the enemy, even his huge dug down Tiger tanks, remained invisible amongst the hedge-topped banks that surrounded the little fields. Here advancing British infantry warily approach the next field in their slow and dangerous progress through the Normandy bocage

Plate 7. On 16 June, only ten days after D-Day, King George VI landed in Normandy to decorate British soldiers awarded medals for bravery. Here he is seen congratulating a Commando corporal. When Hitler came briefly to France next day it was to a conference in his command post at Soissons, much further from the fighting

4 The 'Epsom' Offensive

The British offensive now mounted was code-named 'Epsom', its objective again the encirclement of Caen. The newly landed VIII Corps were to make the main attack, supported by XXX Corps and I Corps. Lieut General Sir Richard O'Connor, who had brilliantly led the armour in Wavell's sensational desert victory in 1940-1, commanded VIII Corps. It consisted principally of 11 Armoured Division and the 15 Scottish Division. The original intention was a main blow with a left hook from the Airborne bridge-head across the River Odon, but Dempsey decided this constricted territory provided insufficient space. He therefore planned for the right hook to carry most weight, swinging round from Fontenay in the west across the rivers Odon and Orne to Bretteville-sur-Laize, due south of Caen, and on to the high ridge at Bourguébus to bestride the Caen–Falaise road. The left hook, meanwhile, was intended to cut the roads leading to Caen from the east and south-east so that the Germans would be forced out of the city or perish therein. The British would then present a very real threat to Paris, to which the Germans must react with all their available armour. Montgomery wanted to ensure that no panzers could challenge the attack the Americans were to make in the St Lô–Coutances area, secretly the main Allied effort. It was precisely according to the plan that Montgomery had propounded to his generals as far back as 7 April.

Whereas in Montgomery's first assault on Caen the majority of the men had been D-Day shock-troops, already battle-hardened in North Africa and Italy, now thousands who had never heard a shot fired in anger were to be involved. They were mostly from the conscript armies raised since 1939, trained and retrained for such a battle as this. The plan required that the

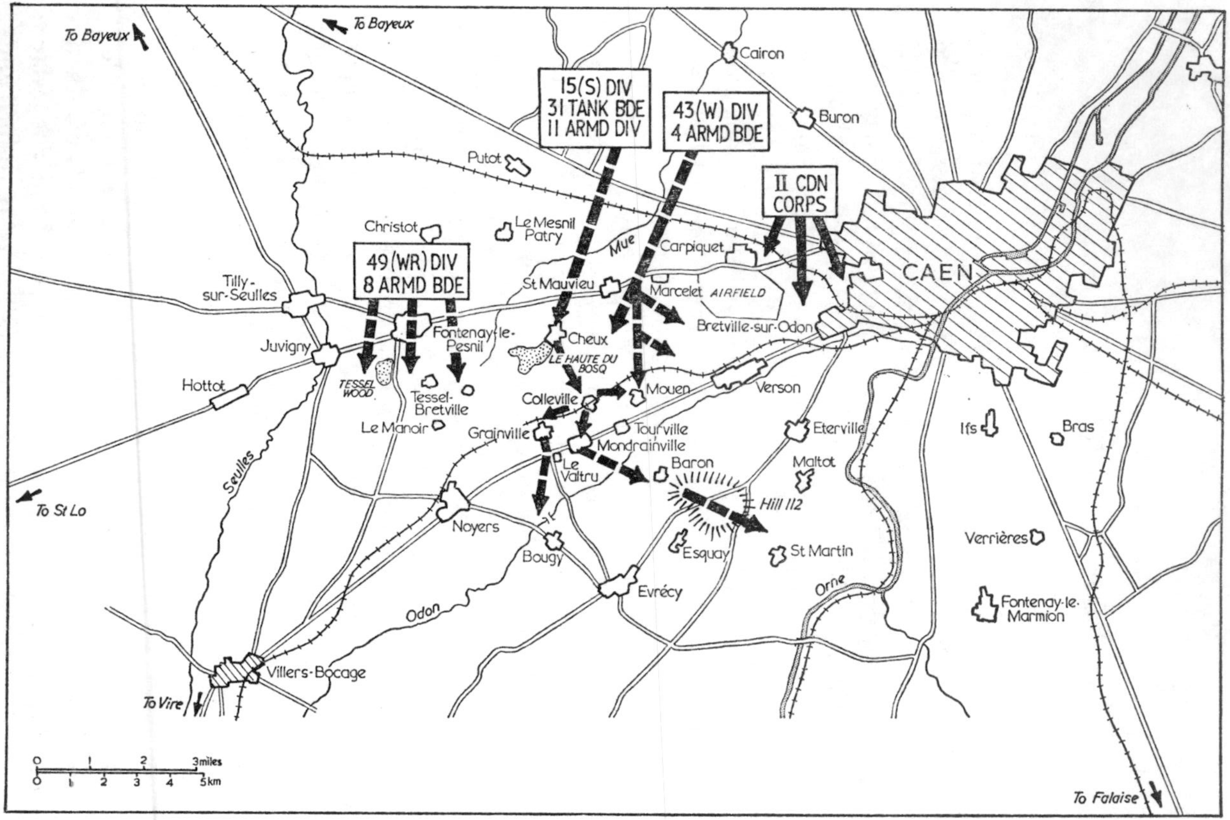

Map 3 'Epsom' 25–28 June

49 West Riding Division and 8 Armoured Brigade of XXX Corps, on the right, should seize the vital high ground of the Fontenay and Rauray ridges. That achieved, the divisions of VIII Corps were to open the main attack in the centre, between Tilly and Caen, across the two rivers. The 15 Scottish Division were to lead, supported by the 31 Tank Brigade and the 4 Armoured Brigade. After they had burst through and established a firm base on the ridge between the Odon and the Orne the infantry of the 43 Wessex Division were to mop up pockets of resistance left behind. The 11 Armoured Division were to execute a rapid left wheel around Caen to establish themselves astride the main Caen–Falaise road where it traversed high ground between Bretteville-sur-Laize and Bourguébus. As these thrusts developed the Canadians of I Corps further left were to advance on Carpiquet airfield while the 51 Highland Division swept forward from the Airborne's Orne bridge-head to capture Ste Honorine and envelop Caen from the other side.

There was good reason to believe that the 'Epsom' offensive must succeed where the first Caen assault had failed. For one thing there were many more men, tanks and guns. In the centre, for instance, VIII Corps had 60,000 men, 600 tanks, 300 guns and the certain support of a further 400 guns from the corps on each side, not to mention the formidable fire-power of the off-shore warships and the bombing power of the Allied air forces. For soldiers going for the first time into battle the knowledge of this immense fire-power was reassuring. To take the full shock of the VIII Corps onslaught in the centre there were only the remnants of the 12 and 26 SS Panzer Regiments, mostly fanatical Nazi teenagers. The line from Fontenay-le-Pesnil through St Marvieu and Cheux eastwards to Carpiquet airfield was held by the 12 SS Panzer Division, considerably depleted in battle. On their left flank they had the support of Panzer Lehr and on their right the 25 SS Panzer Grenadiers directly in the path of the projected Canadian attack. Although wireless intercepts warned the Germans where to expect the heaviest blows they seemed in dire peril. Rommel had the 2 Heavy Tank Company, armed with Tiger tanks, moved in behind the 26 Panzer Regt to confront any break-through.

The 'Epsom' offensive opened in silence by night, the Cameron Highlanders stealing in to Ste Honorine on 23 June to overwhelm the surprised German garrison. A series of bitter enemy counter-attacks were beaten off with the help of the 13/18 Hussars, the Seaforth Highlanders and heavy artillery fire.

John Welch of Swinton, Nr Manchester, was a corporal in the Seaforth Highlanders:

'It was a lovely day when we neared the ridge overlooking Ste Honorine, held by the 6 Airborne Division. It was a gradual exposed slope down to the village. Shells were whining over to the rear and dropping between us and the village as we moved down in extended order. We took cover in the cornfields just before the village but Spandaus were raking our cover and many were wounded. The Camerons must have been putting up a hell of a fight and their walking wounded were coming through us.

'The noise outside Ste Honorine was terrific. Jerry was counter-attacking from the left, infantry and tanks. Our Brens, rifles and anti-tank guns were replying. Our platoon officer and CO were doing a grand job exposing themselves, moving along the line to keep morale up. So far we had done really nothing and to wait, as we were doing, was nerve breaking. Then the order came to move to the edge of the village to cover the Camerons, who were pulling out. Jerry had taken most of the village and I did not fancy our chances in the open against tanks. Then the order was cancelled and we had to stay put to cover the Camerons' withdrawal.

'Time passed. Firing was coming from the village. Then we were told to move back in extended order. Up the slope we went, shells dropping. One chap just disappeared when a shell dropped at his feet. We reached the ridge, now held by our chaps. Once back in a sunken road the tension left me feeling like a wet rag. A rumour of another attack on Ste Honorine was strengthened when a draft arrived late that night. Some were motor transport men filling in as infantry. A new officer had been an artillery officer. I was not looking forward to whatever might be in store. Ste Honorine was to be attacked again, 5 Camerons with 2 Seaforths in support.

'Over the ridge we went again and the Camerons, by now in the village, were meeting stiff opposition. They would be relieved to hear the clank of tanks moving up with us following. The Camerons cleared the village apart from snipers but the wooded areas had caused trouble for one of our platoons, and we were switched to support them. Shells were coming thick and fast. As we entered the wood a machine-gun began firing and we began to leapfrog the sections towards it. German slit trenches, well camouflaged, could be seen. They were occupied. We got down. We had the feeling all was not well, it was too easy. Then white flags were being waved. Jerry had just wiped out one platoon and was now giving himself up? "It's a trick," said the senior NCO, so we attacked. As soon as we moved we came under heavy fire. The trenches were overrun and I must admit no prisoners were taken.

'We moved in to Ste Honorine, advanced up the narrow road and met Camerons coming back. They told us they were being counter-attacked. Shelling was now continuous. Our task now was to get to the road running across our front, swing left and contact the Camerons where most of the firing was. The road was reached and we came to a cross-roads. There we saw an officer standing in a Bren carrier sending messages for artillery support, also about eight chaps resting with their backs to a wall. This sunken road was giving them feelings of false security and we told them so. We moved on. Over the fields, as we looked towards Colombelles, we could see German troops advancing. Shells were dropping very close so we did an about turn. We found the officer in the carrier dead, his driver also, and the soldiers who had been resting were dead or dying. We moved back to Ste Honorine, still being shelled and mortared. We had only enough men left to make one platoon from the three which began the attack.'

On the right, meanwhile, at 4.15am on 25 June, in darkness

and thick mist, infantry of the Royal Scots Fusiliers, York and Lancasters and the Lincolns advanced in extended line behind a tumultuous creeping barrage. In the smoke-thickened fog units began to lose touch as they entered cornfields. Enemy machine-guns opened up through the fog blanket and soon they were involved in vicious hand-to-hand fighting with German infantry, with no quarter given. From this bloody chaos the British emerged victors although they had suffered cruelly. Men of the York and Lancasters were the first to attain their objective, the ridge at Fontenay. But even as they were consolidating three huge tanks, Panthers or Tigers, growled menacingly towards them. With their anti-tank gun the infantry knocked out the first on a bridge, thus blocking the road from Caen, and destroyed the second as it swung away. The third was knocked out by a Sherman tank armed with a 17-pounder gun.

Although some British formations had burst through and reached their objectives at the day's end, the ridge at Rauray was still in enemy hands. General Sepp Dietrich, commanding the I SS Panzer Corps, was nevertheless alarmed by the British penetration and ordered the 2 Heavy Tank Company, the last mobile reserve available to the 12 SS Panzer Division, to counter-attack. This they did at 5.00am on 26 June, shortly before some 600 British tanks attacked on a front of only five kilometres, crushing the panzer grenadiers and pioneers immediately in their path but halting when a furious German artillery barrage erupted behind them to force their supporting infantry to ground. Formations of tanks then set about liquidating pockets of resistance.

The 15 Scottish Division meanwhile moved up to attack their objectives, including the villages of Cheux, St Mauvieu, Grainville-sur-Odon and Colleville. The Odon crossings were also to be seized and a gap forced through which the massed tanks of the 11 Armoured Division would burst to seize the high ground at Baron and the dominating Hill 112. They were then to swing east to capture the crossings over the Orne. But as the force massed by night, heavy rain fell. As zero-hour approached 700 guns began a ferocious bombardment of the enemy. Behind this barrage they moved forward through ravaged villages and churned-up fields.

It was not until late afternoon that the Scots crossed the Caen road still without having come under fire. Great billowing rain clouds darkened the scene, and indeed the weather was so bad that the extensive opening programme of air support had to be cancelled. Then, with startling suddenness, enemy machine-guns opened up on the Scottish infantry among orchards at Le Haut du Bosc. Supporting tanks raked the ground ahead with their fire as attempts were made to advance, but always the enemy machine-guns halted them. Eventually the 'furious Scotsmen' (as German prisoners subsequently described them) took the villages of La Gaule, St Mauvieu, Le Haut du Bosc and Cheux, after savage hand-to-hand fighting. And although Cheux was now in British hands, this shattered village was under heavy enemy shell-fire and heaped rubble and wrecked vehicles blocked the narrow road, slowing the advance of two divisions.

A brigade of Churchills was sent forward to accompany the infantry. When they reached the Caen road, the 11 Armoured Division was to attack. The 23 Hussars and 2 Fife and Forfar Yeomanry, backed by the 3 Royal Tanks, moved up to lead. Some of this armour was supporting an advance on Colleville by the 2 Gordons, but formations were caught up in the traffic block at Cheux. As the leading tanks came up over the ridge they were struck by devastating shell-fire and one after the other they burst into flames. It was a shocking foretaste of the execution to be wrought by the eighty 88mm guns the enemy had been able to bring up here during the three days' gale.

One formation of the British 49 Division involved was the Tyneside Scottish. Robert Nixon of Dundee, then a private, remembers how they were assembled to attack a hill-top wood near Tessel. 'I saw the Sherman tanks go up in confident and steady formation and disappear into the wood,' he recalls. 'I was very scared at the thought of my first action but the sight of the tanks charging into the wood eased my fears, because I thought there would be nothing left to fight. Imagine my dismay when an hour or so later the tanks, or what was left of them, came belting out back.' Later Nixon joined two other soldiers going along a lane flanked by high banks. They were subjected to Spandau fire as they passed a gateway. The other two were wounded and were driven off in a Bren carrier which had just delivered ammunition to the company. Nixon was sent to the brow of a hill to mortar any enemy he saw. When the enemy mortared along a hedge beside him, he was wounded and sent back. 'I learned later that the very same night the battalion was attacked ferociously by Tigers and infantry. Of about twelve Dundee blokes in that company only two of us came out alive.'

By the morning of 26 June there were still enemy holding out in Fontenay, while Rauray was completely in their hands. They were in strength between Tessel Wood and Rauray where some ten Tiger tanks and supporting infantry were well dug-in. A British attack through Le Manoir from Tessel towards Rauray was repulsed by the 12 SS Panzer Regiment. Then panzers were launched eastwards against the breakthrough made by the 15 Scottish and 11 Armoured Divisions. Supported by heavy artillery concentrations the 12 Panzers knocked out a number of British tanks and established positions near Le Haut du Bosc facing towards Cheux. This enemy success coincided with 23 Hussars pulling back behind a hill to refuel and re-arm. Night fell with the rain pouring upon the waterlogged battlefield and constant mortaring made the lot of the halted British infantry even more miserable. Robert Bateson of Windermere, a corporal in the Glasgow Highlanders, was in an orchard under constant mortar fire for four days.

'We were having difficulty getting supplies in and wounded out. It was really sad to see some of your best pals being slaughtered by shrapnel and gun fire. I never expected to get back home. One poor chap got out of his trench and, with teeth clenched and bayonet fixed, he charged towards the enemy. He got riddled with bullets. Like thousands more in those days I many times missed death by inches.'

At the end of the first day of 'Epsom' the Odon had not been reached and the enemy still held most of the high ground. But although Army Group B could record a 'complete defensive success', it had only been achieved by the use of Rommel's last reserves of panzers against the British. The Americans had yet to face even one panzer division. And because the threat posed by the 'Epsom' offensive was causing Rommel such alarm, he ordered that 'everything which can be assembled must be thrown into the fight'. This included a battle group and two brigades of multiple mortars switched from the American sector.

Tom Perry of Walsall, then a private in the Worcestershire Regiment, recalls taking over from the Highlanders in Cheux on 27 June.

'The noise came first. I was sure that a thousand gates on rusty hinges were being opened, the sound amplified a million times. I had never heard the like before. That alone terrified me and I began trying to claw myself further below ground. They were aptly named "moaning minnies", those multi-barrelled mortars! Then they landed. It seemed to me, lying there trembling like a leaf, that every shell Jerry had in France was dropping in our company area. Even now I remember thinking "If I get out of this lot I'll live for years".'

That same day a sadly depleted company of Argyll and Sutherland Highlanders seized an unblown bridge over the Odon at Tournauville, and were followed across by tanks of the 23 Hussars, leading 29 Armoured Brigade. They wheeled south around Carpiquet and headed for Hill 112. A hole six miles wide had been torn in the German line. The 11 Armoured Division's infantry brigade (the 159) and the rest of 29 Armoured streamed across the Odon. But although by the morning of 28 June, VIII Corps had taken its first objective, it was still not possible for Montgomery to concentrate the huge mass of armour and men for a really crushing attack. The bottleneck at Cheux was one of the main reasons. Although a considerable breakthrough had been achieved the extensive armoured

sweep behind the German positions at Caen had not been
executed. Already enemy reinforcements were on the way.
Formations of the 21 Panzer Division, locked in battle with the
Airborne bridge-head since D-Day, were now directed towards
this latest danger point. By evening on 27 June they had
reached Verson, the HQ of General Kurt ('Panzer') Meyer,
under whose direction reinforcements were placed.

On 28 June a battle group of infantry, artillery and tanks
bitterly resisted the next British thrust. Scottish infantry of the
HLI suffered heavy casualties, caught by vicious machine-gun
fire as they advanced confidently across a cornfield. The
Germans launched a ferocious attack along the railway embankment towards Mouen, an objective of the Scots. After the
HLI had been pinned down for a long while and tanks supporting them had been destroyed, one platoon debouched from the
cornfield and got to close quarters. The Scots fought like
demons as they went in with the bayonet and when the Germans
fled they left over fifty dead. A number of panzers were also
destroyed by British tanks and anti-tank guns.

The Scottish salient across the Odon, where by now two
bridges had been captured intact to enable the main strength
of 11 Armoured Division to cross and probe southwards, caused
acute alarm at the German Seventh Army HQ. Col General
Friedrich Dollman, the army commander, was so overwhelmed
by anxiety that he died of a heart attack. As Rommel and von
Rundstedt were now on their way to Berchtesgaden, bidden by
Hitler, the Germans were without their three senior commanders just when they were most needed. The 11 Armoured
Division pushed on towards Esquay and Hill 112, and were
working around north-east of Evrecy, but at nightfall tanks
which had gained isolated positions on high ground were
withdrawn.

Mouen was taken next day by the 1 Worcesters, a battalion
that had not before tasted battle. They did so across a battlefield strewn with dead Germans and soldiers of the HLI and
Monmouths, who had attacked after the Scots infantry's
breakthrough. But the British armour failed to concentrate fast
enough to pour through this gap. The Germans reacted with

much greater speed to bring up panzers and batteries of the dreaded 88mm guns, a number of which were rushed to Hill 112 just in time to repulse Sherman tanks of the 23 Hussars. Next morning, however, a simultaneous attack by British tanks and American Lockheed Lightning fighters threw the German gunners into a fatal confusion. Most of the guns were destroyed and their crews killed and wounded before the Germans withdrew. Artillery fire from Hill 112 was now directed upon every enemy movement.

There was understandable disappointment among the men of 29 Armoured Brigade when they were ordered to withdraw from the hill. They could not know how massive was the enemy counter-attack force now gathering. Dempsey however was all too aware that the Germans had begun to call upon their strategic reserves. Both the 1 and 2 SS Divisions had been identified in the escalating battle, to which it was known the enemy had committed strong elements of six panzer divisions. With stronger flak and fighter protection the enemy columns were pressing forward along almost every road leading to the Odon valley. Dempsey decided to delay the attempted Orne crossing until he had consolidated north of the Odon.

This formidable massing of enemy armour was probed by British armoured-car reconnaissance patrols. How hazardous were such patrols is remembered by Dennis Bunn, of Chelmsford, then with the 15 Scottish Reconnaissance Regiment.

'My feelings on patrol were probably typical. We were the first of a two-car patrol followed up by Bren carriers. I cautiously drove the heavy Humber armoured car, my previous confidence in the armour plating having waned since seeing similar vehicles burned out and overturned like toy cars. Inside the car was intense heat and darkness, outside brilliant sunshine. I sweated and gripped the steering wheel with damp hands as I peered through a small aperture at the ground in front, the high hedge on the right, the ground sloping away to the left, at the trees, the bushes, seeing or suspecting danger in every blade of grass. We passed a headless body in German uniform lying in a gateway. We came on a straight piece of road and approximately 600 yards in front a stone breastwork. Our Besa machine-gun sent a stream of bullets down the road.

'Up to then there had been a dead silence, as there always seemed to be before contact, not even any sound of birds. Then the road, trees, sky, everything was gone and all I could see was red fire and black smoke. Something had exploded immediately in front. The Besa was still going, empty cases rattling behind me. I reversed a few yards. We made our radio report but Command Car informed us it was a stray shell. We moved on forward . . . I can still remember my feelings before the third run. Accept that we will be hit. I pray that my injuries will not be too severe; certainly I hope not more than one leg. I shall be twenty-one tomorrow. I'd like to make it. Forward again. Again that complete blacking out by red fire and black smoke. As it cleared I had a strong feeling of calmness and relief. I was not even scratched! The carrier-borne troops went out on foot to investigate. There was a large anti-tank gun with dug-in German infantry. We lost three killed and five wounded in the ensuing action. As darkness fell we drew back. I could not avoid driving over the bodies of two German soldiers sprawled in the road . . .'

5   A Mounting Unease

At this point in Montgomery's 'Epsom' offensive, it began to appear that the objectives had not been attained. Caen, named as a main D-Day objective, was still untaken on D + 24, and at immense cost. Already a quarter of the British infantry involved had been killed or wounded and hundreds of tanks put out of action. Remembered by William Henry, of Prestwick, Scotland, a signaller with 11 Armoured Division, as his saddest memory, were 'the rows, along the roadside, of dead neatly rolled into shrouds of turf for all the world like so many rolls of linoleum'. He recalls the smell of death that was everywhere. Some British soldiers on this brutal battlefield swore that the stench from German dead was different from the smell of the British and it was possible to discern, just by sniffing the air, who had suffered most casualties in any close-quarters engagement. Robert Boulton, of St Austell, Cornwall, a twenty-year-old private in a carrier platoon of the Queen's, with the 7 Armoured Division, remembers passing through the 43 Infantry Division after an attack: 'One of their battalions had their dead lined up in a field. It really got me, the blanket-wrapped figures so still, their big boots sticking out of the bottom of their blankets.'

The press, both British and American, had begun to reflect a mounting unease. How was it that Montgomery, purportedly the master of the set-piece battle, had failed to break through the German encirclement? Yet Montgomery continued to state publicly, with what his critics took to be an unremitting smugness, that he was getting the enemy 'off balance' entirely according to plan. He had noted that the enemy had committed 21 Panzer, 12 SS and Panzer Lehr Divisions to regain the beaches, and failed. The next step was obviously to seal off the

49

beach-head until a really strong armoured force could be concentrated for a decisive attack. In the period 13–30 June, five more panzer divisions—2 Panzer, 1 SS, 2 SS, 9 SS and 10 SS— had joined in. Their combined effort would have been very formidable but their concentration was never achieved because it was forestalled by heavy British attacks. One by one the panzer divisions had been flung in. The presence of seven panzer divisions (with elements of an eighth)—two-thirds of the enemy armour in France—along a 20 mile front, gave some idea of the heavy fighting in the last week of June, and of the importance which the enemy attached to Caen.

At the extravagant expense of British and Canadian soldiers the 'Epsom' offensive had already achieved outstanding *strategic* results. By comparison, the task of Omar Bradley's US First Army, in breaking out of the Cherbourg Peninsula and capturing the port, was easy going, opposed by only half a panzer division, largely equipped with obsolescent French tanks. The repeated attacks and threats of attacks in the British sector had undoubtedly kept the enemy off balance and at no time had Rommel, that master of the massed panzer attack, been able to concentrate his armour. Despite heavy casualties, 'Epsom' had been good for British morale. The troops felt they could have swept southwards from Hill 112 while repulsing any enemy counter-attacks. Within the wider strategy of the whole war, this offensive had had even more important repercussions. It had drawn in the very German armoured reserve that had smashed the Red Army's spring offensive, so that when the Russian summer offensive opened it was soon effective.

This German armoured reserve, the II SS Panzer Corps, consisting of the 9 and 10 SS Panzer Divisions, had been ordered to strike at the 'Scottish Corridor' from the south-west, the 10 SS at the Odon bridge-head and Hill 112 and the 9 SS towards le Valtru and the Cheux bottleneck. Another SS formation, the 2 SS Panzer Division, sent up from near Toulouse, along with Panzer Lehr, were to strengthen this latter blow. On the other side of the 'Scottish Corridor' the 1 SS Panzer Division, even now arriving from Belgium, was to assist the 12 SS Panzer Grenadier Division and 21 Panzer Division in the attack. The strategic reserve of German armour was being drawn piecemeal into the brutal defensive battle. It had been Hitler's expectation that his massed SS Panzer Divisions, the elite of his armoured forces, would smash through to the sea, to 'Dunkirk' the British again. After such a reverse, and with the people at home cowering beneath the deluge of V1s, the British would surely sue for peace.

In drizzling rain, the British and Canadians prepared to face this massive attack. The *bocage* country where they were dug in must be to their advantage now. The men of the 15 Scottish Division faced westwards from their narrow 'corridor' towards where II SS Panzer Corps was concentrating. The Wessex Division, who had just captured the villages of Marcelet, Mouen and Bas de Mouen, and had cleared the *bocage* terrain southwards to the Odon and pushed a battalion beyond, now lined up along the other side of the corridor. The danger was obviously greatest on the western flank for there the ridge which thrust out past Rauray to Cheux offered a hidden approach for enemy armour. British tanks, anti-tank guns and artillery were therefore massed here.

When the 9 SS Panzer Division attacked, although some tanks did penetrate to Cheux, everywhere the British and Canadian infantry stood firm. The enemy had not been able to begin until 2.30pm instead of the scheduled 7am because of continued attacks by the RAF. In renewed fine weather RAF fighters and fighter-bombers attacked all observed enemy concentrations and columns. The panzer divisions could not bring up their tanks because their fuel lorries had been blown up. By the time the panzers did attack it was already too late. The British guns had massed and subjected them to such heavy fire that only half were able to attack. Some got through to the vicinity of Esquay and Gavrus, at the southern extremity of the corridor, but everywhere the Scots fought back bitterly. These panzers from Russia had never before encountered such devastating artillery fire and air attack.

'We saw masses of German armour moving across our front about three miles away,' remembers Jack Knights, from

North Walsham, manning a 6-pounder of the 61 Anti-Tank
Regt. 'We had orders to remain silent, a good job too I
thought. I did not think our few guns would be much good
against that lot. The German guns opened up in a continuous barrage; it was like standing under a bridge with a
dozen express trains roaring overhead. It lasted for hours
and then suddenly stopped. The attack came in, we could
see the German infantry advancing between the tanks
nearly on top of us. I did not think we stood a chance. We
had been told not to fire until the whistle blew. Then it blew
and we fired our brens and anti-tank guns. But the weight of
fire that came from behind us was tremendous. From miles
away big guns opened up—5.5s, 4.5s, 25-pounders, 4.2
mortars and machine-guns in the fields behind us. We had
the express train again, but going the other way. And we had
thought we were alone . . .'

The bombardments from the warships were particularly
destructive. German Panther tanks were overturned by the
mere blast of a shell from a battleship and massed raids by
RAF heavy bombers were equally devastating. Meanwhile
German troop concentrations and headquarters were shaken
and often dispersed by the point-blank attacks of the rocket-
firing Typhoons, Spitfires and Mustangs of Second Tactical
Air Force. Illustrative of the impact of the great four-engined
British bombers was the fate of a battalion of the 20 Panzer
Grenadier Regiment in a forest near Bas des Forges. They
simply ceased to exist. They had been en route to fall upon the
British traffic-jam at Cheux. A bombing attack was made on
Villers-Bocage with the aim of so blocking the roads that the
panzers would not get through. Waves of four-engined Halifaxes
and Lancasters escorted by Spitfires and Thunderbolts were
sent in, wave upon wave for almost as far as the eye could see.
The air armada included obsolescent four-engined Stirling
bombers, twin-engined Wellingtons and Blenheims, even
Ansons from anti-submarine patrolling and Oxford trainers.
As they discharged their loads on the once-neat little town, it
erupted with great gouts of red-brick dust until it was an un-

Plate 8. Great waves thunder shorewards in the British Mulberry harbour at Arromanches during the terrible gale that lashed the invasion coast for three days. It caused a grave curtailment of supplies and reinforcements

Plate 9. When not attacking through the suicidal small fields of the bocage, British infantry were called upon to advance through wide open corn fields. This is a typical scene at the start of an attack, with a supporting Churchill tank in the foreground. As they go forward these soldiers will be subjected to heavy bombardment by artillery and nebelwerfers and will be raked by the fire of hidden machine guns

Plate 10. A British patrol, alert for the presence of Germans anywhere around, pause in the cover of a hedge before they make a dash to cross a gap which will almost certainly be covered by German Spandaus. This was one of the many dangerous moments in the often brief life of an infantryman in attacks

Plate 11. A typical scene as British infantry, supported by tanks, make an attack across a Normandy cornfield. Invariably the Germans had cut avenues through the often shoulder high corn and along them fired machine guns on fixed lines as the British soldiers were exposed to them. Enemy infantry also lay in wait in slit trenches and fox holes amidst the corn and bloody hand to hand fighting ensued

recognisable ruin shrouded in a towering red fog. Although some panzers were caught in the holocaust it did not prevent newly arrived German armour pushing on. But General Hauser later admitted: 'Hardly had the tanks assembled when they were attacked by fighter-bombers. This disrupted the troops. The murderous fire from the naval guns in the Channel and the terrible British artillery destroyed the bulk of our attacking force in its assembly area.'

Already aware that his counter-offensive was getting nowhere, Hauser suggested withdrawal from Caen to 'husband the resources of the panzer divisions and create a defensive line commensurate with our infantry strength'. But Lieut General Hans Speidel (Rommel's chief-of-staff) said this would be ordered only 'as soon as authorisation is received from Supreme Command'. Any hope of this happening had already been vetoed by Hitler who brushed aside Rommel's assertion that the British 'Epsom' offensive had only been stopped by committing the entire German strategic reserve. He scorned a warning that the Seventh Army would be utterly destroyed and the Fifteenth Army powerless to prevent invasion at the Pas de Calais. When von Rundstedt afterwards told Field Marshal Wilhelm Keitel, Chief of Supreme Command, that the only thing left to do was to make peace, Keitel reported this to Hitler who immediately replaced von Rundstedt with Field Marshall Gunther von Kluge. A favourite of Hitler, von Kluge had commanded the Fourth Army that so dramatically charged through France to the Channel coast in 1940 and played a leading role in the German advance to the gates of Moscow.

As the German counter-attack persisted, the Argylls came under heavy attack in the Odon bridgehead near Gavrus, but held on. During the night of 1/2 July, a newly arrived division, the 53 Welsh Infantry, was sent to relieve the battle-weary Scots. Three times that day powerful enemy infantry attacks had been made on this sector and each time had failed before the fire of the British infantry and massive bombardment by twelve regiments of artillery. When the attacks moved across to the Baron sector, they were similarly stopped. Heavy losses were also sustained by an enemy attack on a $1\frac{1}{2}$-mile front

D

stretching from near Grainville towards Rauray. Although tanks and infantry penetrated the British forward positions under cover of smoke they were hunted down and destroyed.

Typical of the experiences of British infantrymen were those of Frederick Spencer, of Durham, then a nineteen-year-old corporal in the Durham Light Infantry. The Durhams had fought forward in the 'Epsom' offensive, outflanking Tilly-sur-Seulles, and Spencer's company had advanced through a wood in the teeth of bitter German resistance:

'During the next few days, we sat it out, exposed to air bursts, moaning minnies, snipers and mortar fire. At night it was standing patrols in the valley on our right flank to prevent infiltration by German patrols. The worst hazard was getting back to the safety of our slit trenches before first light. Our positions were on a forward facing slope and we were harassed each day by an 88mm SP gun which came forward to fire at us at very close range.'

Spencer's company was ordered to advance to take a start line from which another DLI company would attack:

'We advanced in extended order in front of a squadron of Sherman tanks. I don't know which was the more disconcerting, the sniper fire from the front or the replies from the tank guns in our rear. The tanks moved through and about 400 yards to our front came under fire from 88mm guns. I saw at least three blow up, followed by the machine-gunning of crew trying to escape. We spent a most uncomfortable time under fire from snipers who had tied themselves into some poplar trees. Some accurate retaliatory fire left several hanging. After dark we were placed among some really thick hedgerows and were told to dig in. As dawn was breaking the sentry pointed out some men some 150 yards to our right front. We came under mortar, shell and machine-gun fire and German infantry advanced.

'Crouching in our shallow holes we replied with rifle and bren and the infantry ran out of the field on to a hidden sunken road. They tried repeatedly to get at us but we drove them back. A little later I heard the creaking of tank tracks. My heart sank. A Tiger rumbled up the sunken road and stopped at a gap in the hedge about 150 yards away. The tank fired several shells into the bank behind our ditch then moved on and engaged the section on my right. I could hear screams coming from that direction. The tank then moved away and after a spell we were attacked by infantry. I fired the bren and we got them back into the sunken road. During this engagement our two company snipers killed a machine-gunner and a man with a grenade thrower creeping along the ditch towards my section. In the sunken road I found a large number of dead Germans.'

The expertise of the DLI riflemen was demonstrated to Robert Mawson, of Consett, Co Durham, then a despatch rider with the 86 Field Regt, RA.

'It was like hell let loose and everybody was on edge. I had to relieve myself and I went into the hedgerow and saw an infantryman who said "Keep down, there is a sniper in that tree. Hold on, I will get him." And he did; the sniper dropped like a stone. As I looked over the hedge I saw around a hundred Bosch, some sitting, some lying but all dead. I asked the infantryman about them and he said "We have to make good our losses," and he never batted an eyelid. Soon after this the chain came off my motor cycle and I was busy with it when someone tapped me on the shoulder. I nearly jumped six feet. It was a German giving himself up! He even helped me with the chain. I told him to get on the back and took him several miles to a prisoner of war cage— I made sure he didn't get shot.'

The panzers had suffered such crippling losses that General Speidel reported: 'The attack by II SS Panzer Corps has been stopped by very strong artillery concentrations.' When his armour was blasted back by the British guns a commander of the 9 SS Panzer Division quoted Dante to end his report:

'Abandon hope all ye who enter here.' Yet another attack, for which infantry in troop-carrying vehicles formed up at Quende-ville, was annihilated by machine-gun, artillery and mortar fire. The battlefield was littered with enemy dead and dozens of their wrecked tanks. Although the British had also suffered heavy casualties, their line was unbroken. The SS panzer divisions had sustained a shattering defeat.

6 Poor Bloody Infantry

Although the Germans had managed to reoccupy Hill 112 and Gavrus, this was only because General Dempsey had withdrawn his armour. Hauser admitted defeat in a message to Rommel's HQ. 'The counter-offensive by 1 and 2 Panzer Corps has had to be temporarily suspended in the face of intensive enemy artillery fire and supporting fire of unprecedented ferocity from naval units. The tenacious enemy resistance will prevent our counter-offensive from having any appreciable effect.' The Battle of the Odon had compelled the enemy hurriedly to commit his armoured reserves, and they had been defeated. At the height of the battle Montgomery had withdrawn his own armour into reserve in such a concentration that it threatened a major offensive on the Caen sector. Thus Rommel, although aware that the Americans were about to launch a major assault, was powerless to challenge them. Montgomery's directive to Bradley now was: 'First US Army will pivot on the left in the Caumont area and swing southwards and eastwards to the general line Caumont–Vire–Mortain–Fougères.' Thence one American corps was to wheel right into the Britanny peninsula while the rest of the army swept forwards south of the *bocage* country to Le Mans–Alençon. The American attack was to open on 3 July, with 4 full corps of 14 divisions against 6 German divisions on a 50-mile front.

The Canadians meanwhile were poised to attack Carpiquet, to free the western exits from Caen. Carpiquet airfield had been converted into a formidable last bastion of the Caen defences. The 21 SS Panzers and the 26 SS Panzer Grenadier Regiment were responsible for holding it, even though thin on the ground. Some forty German tanks sent to reinforce were at-

59

tacked by rocket-firing Typhoons. Set to attack the airfield were the Canadian 8 Infantry Brigade plus a battalion of the Royal Winnipeg Rifles, supported by tanks of the Fort Garry Horse and flame-throwing and flail tanks of the British 79 Armoured Division. These were backed by the concentrated firepower of 428 guns and again the warships, including 16-inch guns of the battleship *Rodney* and the monitor *Roberts'* 15-inch guns. So savage had been the attrition to which the German armour was subjected that Meyer could allocate no more than two or three tanks, hidden in hangars on the airfield. But, although by comparison with the attacking force the defenders were sparse, the panzer grenadiers were in strongly constructed underground blockhouses linked into a formidable fortification.

Soon after 3am on 4 July a thunderous artillery bombardment opened up on the German positions and the attack went in. A retaliatory German barrage caused serious casualties in the Canadian assembly area in a forest near Marcelet. The Chaudiers and North Shore Regiments both suffered heavily at Carpiquet village, captured after bitter hand-to-hand fighting, but tanks which entered the airfield were knocked out by 88mm guns. The Germans subjected the village to an incessant heavy bombardment which pinned the Canadians down. Bad weather grounded the air forces until late afternoon, when RAF Typhoons rocketed panzers dug down at the east end of the airfield. During the night I SS Panzer Corps sent in a determined assault which raged until 8.ooam next morning, penetrating some Canadian positions. The Typhoons returned to the attack, however, and British and Canadian guns heavily bombarded the enemy to kill many and destroy some tanks. By midday Panzer Group West was reporting failure to recapture Carpiquet airfield but the Canadians were still held there on 6 July.

A subsequent night attack by German infantry was defeated by rough, tough French-Canadians, fighting at close quarters with knives. Their ferocity was inspired by reports that the Germans were executing Canadian prisoners. 'French-Canadians returning from Carpiquet told us terrible stories about Germans

murdering prisoners,' recalls Bertram Arnold, of Reading, a
CSM in the Royal Berkshires, who were in support. 'They said
Canadians had been tied to posts and used for bayonet practice.
Really it was good for morale because it made you say "Just
wait until we get at the bastards!" German prisoners were
scared stiff that they were going to be killed.' On both sides the
often desperate fighting men seemed determined on the utter
destruction of the enemy and nothing else. As the bulk of the
Germans whom the British and Canadians were now meeting
were soldiers of the fanatically Nazi SS, this was understandable.

On the evening of 7 July with Carpiquet still not captured,
the first move in a new plan to take Caen by head-on assault
was made. The ravaged city was to be cleared to the banks of
the Orne for bridge-heads to be established to the south.
Montgomery was determined to keep the 2 SS Panzer Corps
committed to the brutal slogging match so that the Americans
could attack untroubled by enemy armour. The identification
of elements of 2 SS Panzer Division in the American sector had
given cause for alarm. New infantry divisions identified on the
British front were obviously there to relieve the panzers. 1 and
2 SS Division, 21 Panzer Division and Panzer Lehr had been
withdrawn, wholly or partially, obviously for a massive armoured blow against the Americans. Montgomery knew that he
must immediately re-involve this armour against the British
and Canadians. If they now, without any pause to lick their
wounds, were to launch an attack to which the Germans were
compelled to react, that would achieve Montgomery's object.
Such an attack would be one to gain the high ground south of
Bourguébus, to threaten the lateral routes south of Caen. The
important communication centres of Falaise and Argentan
were objectives which the enemy must desperately defend.
First, however, Caen must be in British hands.

The frontal assault on Caen was to begin with a heavy
bomber raid that was to rouse much controversy. The plan,
Operation 'Charnwood', was typical of Montgomery, with three
divisions numbering 115,000 men going in behind a tremendous artillery barrage directed upon a target presumably already

virtually destroyed. It was known the enemy had created a formidable defence line across the approaches to Caen where a series of villages, with steel and concrete strongpoints, had been transformed into a linked underground fortress line. Deep mine-fields and many tank obstacles rendered this line virtually tank-proof. Unfortunately the air bombardment was timed for between 9.50pm and 10.30pm on 7 July with the attack not until 4.20am next morning. The huge bomber raid could not fail to convince the enemy that it must be the overture to an overland assault. The reason was said to be a doubtful weather forecast, but events did not bear this out.

First the massive guns of the battleship *Rodney* hurled 29 shells 25,000 yards on to the key hill at Point 64 where the roads from Epron and Lebisey converged before running down to Caen. Some 500 Lancasters and Halifaxes were then despatched to drop 2,560 tons of bombs upon the northern outskirts. The given bombing line was 6,000 yards ahead of the British forward positions as a safety margin. It meant, however, that this huge mass of high explosives would fall three miles *behind* the main fortified German defence positions, because the British front line was so close, upon an area where the Germans had no significant defences. Dempsey hoped it would create a wilderness through which no enemy reinforcements would be able to reach the front. It was planned for the immense ensuing artillery bombardment, including the warships, to fall upon the forward enemy positions.

Through the last glowerings of daylight on 7 July the British troops tautly awaiting their zero hour were heartened by a swelling roar from the north which developed into a seemingly endless stream of four-engined bombers heading for Caen. They flew on into the black curtain of anti-aircraft shell bursts, glittering at lower levels with probing streams of tracers. How the RAF Pathfinders first set the scene is remembered by Frederick Wilkinson, of Manchester, a corporal with a Typhoon wing on an advanced airfield: 'It had been a beautiful day and very hot. As the Pathfinders moved in it was one of the most magnificent sights I have ever seen. The chandeliers began to hang in space until soon there were yellowy-green lights, hundreds of them, standing motionless and lighting up the whole of Caen and outlying districts. Then the bombs began to fall.' The ground trembled as spout after spout of smoke and flame leaped up from the ancient city. Soon it was entirely obliterated by a great soaring curtain of smoke and dust, which spread out to blacken the skies above the waiting British and Canadian troops, up to three or four miles away. But still the bombers came on remorselessly launching yet more bombs into the holocaust. There were however very few enemy in Caen.

The strong defences at the city's approaches remained virtually intact. Upon them early next day the immense British artillery barrage fell, yet the Germans were ready and in strength when the infantry came in. On the left were the British 3 Infantry Division, now set to advance parallel to the River Orne to capture Lebisey and Herouville, their actual D-Day objectives. They reached both within one hour. In the centre was 59 Division, which had not yet seen action. They, too, were soon in the outskirts of their first objectives, La Bijude and Galmache. On the right were the Canadian 3 Infantry Division, some already involved at Carpiquet, supported by the flail and flame-throwing tanks of 79 Armoured Division, plus two Canadian armoured brigades. The two experienced flanking divisions soon outdistanced the 59 which became embroiled in heavy fighting against the crack 12 SS. La Bijude, where the Germans had formidably deep trenched defence systems with dug-down Tigers, changed hands twice before it was captured.

Dennis Hischier, of Chislehurst, Kent, then a corporal in the 141 Regt, RAC (The Buffs) went into this attack in a Churchill 'Crocodile' flame-thrower tank:

'The previous evening we were just finishing off a repair when I noticed an old woman coming up the hill . . . She was dressed all in black, a real 'old crone' type. She came right up to me and stared into my eyes intently, and did the same to my gunner and wireless operator. Then, as my driver and flame gunner arrived, she did the same to them, then grabbed both of them round their necks and cried and cried over them. They were most embarrassed and eventually

managed to escape from her clutches. She went back down
the hill, still sobbing. A feeling of dread came over me.

'Early next morning we moved up, to the fire of massed
artillery and mortars. We experienced a very heavy German
counter-bombardment. The South Staffs infantry ran into
very heavy fire from the trench system near La Bijude. There
were strong anti-tank positions there, as we had feared.
Later we crossed the start line behind a troop of Sherman
flails. My troop leader noticed our infantry had not joined
in behind so we were ordered back. Unfortunately this had
primed Jerry that an attack was imminent and the shelling
was extremely heavy. Once again we set out and saw our
flail was well on the way to the railway embankment. As the
flail turned to one side I went up over the embankment,
heart in mouth as my thin underbelly showed briefly. Then
we were among the trenches. I gave a long squirt of flame up
the left-hand one, saw my troop leader close to me just the
other side of the right-hand trench. The turret gunner was
using the Besa to good effect when he had a double feed. I
told him to use the 75mm on HE and gave him gun control.
He scored a hit some 100 yards ahead in a low bush in which
something blew up.

'Jerry helmets showed in the trench in front and the flame
thrower swept along it. Then my face hit the periscope and a
sheet of flame flung me into the bottom of the turret. I
couldn't breathe as the flames roared out of the driving
compartment. Struggling upwards I somehow pushed the
hatches open, lifted myself up. The gunner and wireless operator were following me so I rolled over the side of my tank
and flattened myself to the ground, looking for the driver to
appear. But we had been hit by a 75mm through the flame-
thrower mounting and both driver and flame-thrower gunner had been killed instantly. As my other two crewmen
joined me grenades came sailing over us. We promptly rolled
into the right-hand trench. I then realised how badly we
were burned, unable to use our pistols. We started crawling
back, using our elbows as our hands were so painful. I was
able to pick out a large tree on our start line to get my line.

Then we were back among the infantry. That finished the fighting war for me, but I have often wondered how that old woman knew who in my crew were going to die, because I am sure she did know.'

The South Staffords pushed on through La Bijude towards Caen but were stopped before Malan. The British 3 Division, however, faced by a weaker Luftwaffe division just brought in from Holland, had managed to fight through to the fringe of Caen's bombed northern suburbs. It was to find an almost impassable barrier of massive craters and mountains of rubble, with streets choked with the huge blocks of stone with which Caen's older buildings were constructed. There was no chance of armoured columns thrusting through to seize the bridges across the Orne. Bulldozers would have to go in first. Soldiers could hear the faint groans and stirrings of French civilians beneath the mountains of debris.

Throughout all this fighting the plunging Allied fighters and medium bombers fiercely attacked enemy strongpoints, gun areas, headquarters, forming-up places, bridges, roads and railways. And the *Rodney* sent 16-inch shells at 32,000 yards range among 35 panzers about to enter the battle. Several were shattered, the rest fled. The Canadians meanwhile, with the full weight of the artillery now switched to their front, fought forward strongly to attack Buron, Authie and Franqueville, passing Carpiquet where the Panzer Grenadiers were still holding out. Soldiers of the 12 SS Panzer Division dug down amidst the ruins of Buron were prepared to fight to the death and it took nearly all that day to liquidate them. German tanks came at the Canadians again and again through the smoke and the rubble but were blasted at point-blank range. One Canadian 17-pounder anti-tank battery was credited with the destruction of 13 panzers. On both sides the casualties were heavy.

At Ginchy the Canadians triumphed after a fierce fight decided by a massed charge of 16 Bren carriers, all guns firing. They surged on to take Authie and St Louet, to observe the enemy pulling back from Carpiquet. This prompted them to push on into Franqueville. 'Early next morning we moved down the road from Franqueville towards the Caen–Bayeux highway,' recalls James McDonald, of the Glengarries. 'When we got to the junction an officer with lots of braid and red directed us to turn left. I later learned our point man was none other than Major General Crocker. You had to admire a man like that who would go right to the front.' Maintaining the momentum the Canadians fought their way on into Cussy and captured the village of Ardenne.

On 9 July Malan, another fortress village with dug-down Tigers, was taken by the North Staffords. In the bitter fighting the North Staffords suffered 25 per cent casualties, a figure typical of most infantry units involved. Indeed, there was already a disturbing shortage of British infantry for the very reason that, after five years of war, Britain just did not have sufficient men. Only Britain and Germany had been in the war from the very beginning and both now were suffering manpower shortages. The Normandy slaughterhouse was swallowing up the infantry. The expenditure of flesh and blood in the present battle for Caen was cause for alarm, for Germans as well as British. In this lovely summer weather it was not unusual for an infantryman to wonder at each sunset whether he would ever live to see another, and at each dawn whether that would be his last.

'Normandy was a place where everything was dead, bodies all over the place and a stink of death,' is how Leslie Cornwell of Mansfield, a private in the Durham Light Infantry, remembers it. 'It was like living on the moon, all bomb craters. We lived in slit trenches and at first weren't allowed to make a dugout or funk hole ... Really, I suppose, we lived like frightened rabbits. At certain times one had to stand up, stick your rifle and bayonet out in front, and advance. Jerry would then rain mortars down and half the battalion would get killed and wounded. We were nearly all teenagers and by this time were all bomb happy. Always reduced in numbers to three or four to a section and no way to get out of it except being buried or on a stretcher. Makeshift graves were everywhere. The pioneer platoon even started making white crosses ready for use. Sometimes before attacks you could see "blood waggons" (ambulances) lining up ready and your stomach would turn over.

'I remember the cornfields; everyone would suddenly disappear when the shelling started. The orchards, all full of sour apples, and they were death traps, always a target for mortars. Everyone admitted saying a prayer; just press your nose into the ground, fists clenched, and pray. That was the only answer to shell fire. Yet one would still stand up and run towards the Jerry line without a thought of small arms. Lads laughed when they got slight wounds—anything to get out of it. The first six weeks all sick and wounded went back to Blighty. About two or three came back within weeks and were amazed to find only a few of us they knew. I thought that if by some fluke I survived and went back to England there would be no young men walking about at all because they were all being killed and wounded in Normandy.'

7 The Holocaust of Caen

Caen was now held on the right by an infantry division which had recently replaced the 21 Panzer Division, and in the centre by what remained of the Hitler Jugend Division. The order from Hitler was that not a yard of ground was to be yielded. But on 9 July Meyer ordered his Caen troops back to the southern industrial suburbs of Colombelles and Faubourg de Vaucelles, behind a river barrier. He also withdrew the last surviving young panzer grenadiers from Carpiquet airfield. Although the British 59 Division was still some miles from the city, the British infantry from the east and Canadians from the west were closing in fast. What little remained of Caen was finally taken at dusk and only snipers and a few pockets of desperate resistance remained to be liquidated.

Involved in one of a number of vicious engagements with such pockets was Duncan Kyle, from Ontario, with the Glengarries:

'Suddenly we were in a savage fight. We opened up with Brens and rifles. I swung my rifle slightly to the right, I was staring into the face of a blond SS soldier. He was on his belly, facing me. Our eyes locked. I squeezed the trigger a split second after he raised himself on to his elbows. The ·303 slug caught him just below the throat. The impact lifted his body and he hung in the air for an instant. He was still staring straight into my face. A pool of blood was forming on the pavement under his chest. He looked sleepy, his head nodding. He was still on his elbows and was waving his hands, but not so frantically. He was dying. I think about him often. When he saw me take aim he had started waving his hands in a gesture of surrender . . .'

The continued German defence of the factory area and suburbs across the river, over which every bridge had been blown,
meant that the through routes required to maintain the British
thrust were still inaccessible. Caen itself had lost an estimated
6,000 of its men, women and children. Parts of decaying human
bodies could be seen protruding from the rubble and everywhere the air was foul with the stench of rotting flesh. British
Royal Engineers were early into Caen to try to make it at least
possible to move through. Arthur Wilkes, of Bilston, West
Midlands, was a sapper with 553 Coy, RE:

'My first thoughts as we reached the outskirts were that the
end of the world had come. Mountains of debris towered
twenty or thirty feet high, sewers and service pipes had been
blown on to the surface, cellars smouldered beneath the
ruins. The dead lay everywhere, some scattered about on the
ground, in the gutters, on the footpaths and over the race-
course at the edge of the town. The occasional body floated
in the river. The smell was a mixture of damp plaster, charred
timber and scorched corpses of the people trapped in the
cellars. As we settled in we realised that an area of roughly
thirty square miles had suffered fearful devastation. Every
town and village was ruined or burnt out. Every bridge was
wrecked, railway tracks destroyed, canals choked with debris.
The fields were full of dead cattle, swollen to enormously
distorted shapes, the corn burnt black, the ground seared and
scarred with tank tracks. A few miles to the east of Caen we
came to the shattered village of Tilly le Campagne, where
nothing was standing above knee high. In the middle of the
ruins was an old pram. On the other side were flat, open
fields littered with burnt out tanks, guns swung round at
crazy angles, and the fields were covered with, not corpses,
just the remains, fingers, a hand, a head, and pathetic personal belongings, a bottle of aspirins, rosary beads, torn and
mud-soaked letters, helmets, a prayer book . . .'

The savage fighting for Caen had cost the British I Corps
3,500 casualties, and the British 59 and Canadian 3 Divisions
over 1,000 each. Around eighty tanks had been knocked out.

German casualties had been heavy too, the infantry strength of
the 12 SS Panzer Division, for instance, being reduced to one
battalion. While the bulk of the German armour had been
embroiled with the British and Canadians, the Americans had
made the most of their opportunities. Nevertheless, the American break-out offensive was still very much bogged down and
Cherbourg port was not yet operational. Bradley had instructed
the US VIII Corps to attack southwards against strongly entrenched German positions in thickly wooded hills around the
vital road junction of La Haye-du-Puits. Hitler had ordered his
troops to fight to the death and this they did, losing from one
and a half to two battalions of infantry per day beneath the
massive bombardment of American guns. However, the three
complete German infantry divisions, with the remnants of
three divisions (totalling the strength of one) withdrawn from
the Cotentin peninsula, continued effectively to bar the way.
Since the attack that was to develop into the great American
break-out had begun on 3 July they had advanced considerably
less than one mile per day through hazardous *bocage* and
spreading swamps.

On 6 July General Patton had crossed the Channel secretly
to the Cotentin peninsula. The American front was no further
forward than a line from Caumont in the east across to the
west coast of the Cotentin peninsula by La Haye-du-Puits.
Hitler meanwhile had instructed von Rundstedt to attack 'not
the strength, but the weakness of the enemy west of the Vire
where weaker American forces are located on a broad front'.
His plan was to drive the Americans into the sea 'with four or
five armoured divisions'—now bloodily embroiled with the
British and Canadians. Von Rundstedt and Rommel had been
ordered to Berchtesgaden where General Jodl, chief of the
High Command Operations Staff, noted that 'We are now
compelled to ward off the English attack, instead of counter-
attacking.' Eisenhower had been urging Bradley to 'rush the
preparations for the attack to the south'. The almost total
commitment of the panzer divisions to the British sector had
enabled the United States First Army to reorganise and regroup virtually undisturbed.

Plate 12. A British soldier warily approaches the body of a German sniper, earlier shot down from his vantage point up a tree. In the wooded bocage the enemy snipers, who tied themselves to tree trunks high up amidst thick foliage, proved particularly lethal

Plate 13. Teenage German soldiers who have just been captured. Some of the young Panzer Grenadiers who fiercly resisted the Canadian attacks on Carpiquet airfield were no older than this but, indoctrinated with the Nazi creed from childhood, they fought fanatically

Plate 14. Everywhere amidst the brutal bocage battlefield there were the hasty grave mounds of slain soldiers. Here the names of fallen British infantrymen are being painted on the crosses that will be erected over their temporary graves. Before a big attack the pioneers in infantry formations would make a supply of crosses, which was little encouragement for the young soldiers about to go into action

The British and American armies now in Normandy were each between fifteen and sixteen divisions. But whereas the British only had six divisions waiting to cross from England the Americans had nine there and many more mustering in the United States ready to sail direct to France as soon as ports were available. It had always been Montgomery's plan that when the British and Canadians had drawn the panzer divisions on to them the American army, with its far bigger reinforcements streaming in behind it, would deliver the main Allied punch. The brutal battlefield of Caen would be the firm hinge on which the American attack would swing.

The very fact that the Americans had not yet launched this attack meant that the British and Canadians were having to fight even harder, for the German loss of Caen had driven them to despatch an increasing number of Tigers to that murderous front. The British, even as in North Africa before Montgomery arrived with a superiority of arms and numbers, were grievously outgunned and out-tanked. Again it was a case of the British land cruisers against the German land battleships. The newly arrived Tiger formations were largely manned by experienced tank crews, with supporting grenadier units, from the Russian front. To keep the German armour away from the Americans Montgomery opened up a further offensive, codenamed 'Operation Jupiter', on 10 July. The principal objective was the soaring Hill 112, south-west of Caen. The battle for Normandy appeared to have reached crisis point. The Allies were still hemmed into a seventy-mile wide bridge-head nowhere more than twenty miles deep. Despite their massive frontal assaults at Caen the British and Canadians seemed to have been fought to a standstill, yet had failed to take the heights south of Caen which dominated the battlefield.

On the American front there was an equally frustrating stalemate. Meanwhile, despite the often devastating intervention of Allied air power, and sabotage and ambushes by the French *Maquis* guerrillas, German infantry reinforcements from the south of France were increasingly reaching the battlefield. Continued bad weather was both limiting the Allied capacity to reinforce across the Channel and to operate aircraft from Eng-

E

lish bases. There was now outspoken criticism of Montgomery's conduct of the battle at SHAEF (Supreme HQ Allied Expeditionary Force), in Whitehall and in Washington. The press, particularly in America, was beginning to suggest that Montgomery's methods were threatening the American and British armies with involvement in a campaign that could be as long drawn out, inconclusive and murderous as World War I. Even Eisenhower now expressed misgivings. Omar Bradley, however, was to write: 'Montgomery was spending his reputation in a bitter siege against the old university town of Caen. But had we attempted to exonerate Montgomery by explaining how successfully he had hoodwinked the German by diverting him towards Caen from the Cotentin, we would have given our strategy away. We desperately wanted the Germans to believe this attack on Caen was the main Allied effort.' Patton, meanwhile, lost few opportunities of deriding the apparent British failure. His critical comments were even echoed by his Negro orderly, Sergeant George Meeks, who remarked to Patton before an audience: ' 'Fore God General, that Montgomery is going to grow grass and limpets on his left foot if he don't pull it out of the water.'

One significant difference between the American and the British commanders was that few, if any, American generals had experienced the horrifying slaughter of the trench warfare of World War I. They knew virtually nothing, from personal experiences at any rate, of those murderous conditions. Most of the British generals, and certainly Montgomery, had fought as young officers, many being wounded, where an offensive inevitably doomed tens of thousands of young soldiers to death daily. In their determination to ensure that this did not happen again now, they preferred the carefully prepared set-piece attack, so much Montgomery's *forté*, with massive air and artillery support, to any suggestion of a death or glory charge. By contrast, from Eisenhower down, the American commanders preferred to attack all along the line and all the time, confident that with their huge mechanical resources and manpower they must triumph.

Patton himself had emerged from America's brief participation in World War I covered in glory. In September 1918, when the Germans were on the run, he became a one-man charge, his tank fast outdistancing all the rest of his command. To reluctant American infantry he bellowed: 'Come on, you yellow-bellied bastards! Get up and let's go!' At this point Patton was wounded and put out of that war. Now in July 1944 he was prepared to hurl insults at the British for apparently going to ground like his American infantrymen in 1918, and at Montgomery in particular.

Montgomery, meanwhile, was well satisfied with the Germans' massive concentration of armoured strength on the British front. He remained convinced that so much of the enemy's strength had been sapped by the blood-letting and destruction there that the Americans would soon be able to break out dramatically with no danger of panzers. And despite the growing American impatience with his methods, Montgomery himself remained patient when Bradley informed him on 10 July that he could not launch his offensive until he had amassed far bigger supplies of ammunition and had established a firm jumping-off ground. He would require to force the enemy back beyond the St Lô–Periers Road, but not for another ten days. Montgomery accepted this, even though it meant the British and Canadians having to face the full strength of the German armour for another ten days. Already they had been doing it for five weeks. To continue became inevitable when three of the four German infantry divisions up from the south were also put in the line against the British.

The sort of savage action in which British infantry were continually involved was one in which Frederick Spencer, of the Durhams, fought when attacking the Jurigny–Hottot road on 11 July:

'Our support was flame-throwing Crocodile tanks, our objective some farm buildings surrounded by orchards on the right flank of the main advance. As it was the turn of my section to lead I was stuck out in front, feeling very vulnerable. It seemed a long way across the fields but I could see a hedge on fire near the farm. There was no sign of the tanks and Germans were moving about in the hedgerows. They did not shoot at us and I had no intention of being the first to start, being so exposed. As soon as I stepped on to a track which ran along the perimeter of the farm a deluge of mortar bombs landed amongst us. I felt a terrible pain in my right elbow, was deafened and blown up into the hedge. All around was a shambles. There were one or two heaps of smouldering rags which were dead men. One man was running in circles, blinded. Another was lying on his face and I could see parallel gouges, like tramlines, across his back . . . Another was sitting quietly against the hedge with his right leg blown off at the thigh. There was no sign of the rest of the platoon but minutes later I heard small arms fire to the front and the platoon sergeant and several others came staggering back. There were only six of us left, and we got into positions behind a hedge overlooking the farm. Eventually we were withdrawn.'

The German infantry were obviously there to release panzers to attack the Americans. Montgomery knew he had to do something drastic to involve this armour. He chose to launch a bold attack aimed at establishing British armour on the Bourguébus Ridge, which would menace the Germans with the prospect of a British drive for Paris. Into the attack went the 43 Wessex Division, the 46 Highland Brigade, a brigade of the Canadian 3 Division, the 4 Armoured Brigade and the 31 Tank Brigade. The way ahead was blasted by a massive artillery bombardment. The main road from Caen to Evrecy crossed the flat top of Hill 112, three-quarters of a mile long with the straggling village of Eterville on the way up. Before an advance could be made from the Odon to the Orne, the British had to hold Hill 112, now virtually the key to the whole Normandy battlefield, at the southern extremity of the difficult *bocage* country. It looked out over the wide open landscape, ideal country for massed tank attack, that stretched away to the south.

A preliminary armoured car reconnaissance had suggested that there might be no enemy on the hill, and a platoon of the Royal Welch Fusiliers was sent out to investigate. In fact the enemy were on the hill in strength, and the platoon walked into the trap. As a result the hill was subjected to a heavy artillery barrage. Close behind the pre-dawn barrage came rocket-firing Typhoons to blast German tanks up on the hill, indicated by red smoke shells. The British began to advance along the valley of the Odon, through Verson, Mouen and Baron. The 129 Brigade on the right and 130 Brigade on the left were to capture the hill. Then fast tanks and tracked vehicles, loaded with infantry, were to race for the Orne bridges. But already Tigers had formidably deployed to bar the way. At the village of Maltot, nestling in the Orne valley, the first objective of the inexperienced 130 Brigade, a troop of Tigers were dug down behind hedges in orchards. Soon shattered British tanks were burning in the fields and the attack disintegrated. Next the Tigers set out to establish themselves on Hill 112 with some panzer grenadiers. A British attack by the Duke of Cornwall's Light Infantry was intended to attain precisely the same objective, setting out half-an-hour later. A British artillery OP tank had already driven on to the top of the hill, from which devastating fire was swiftly brought down upon the approaching Tigers. A choking smoke-screen intended to hide the attacking DCLI rolled up and the Tigers ground to a halt at the foot of the hill.

Behind the smoke the British infantry reached the main road across Hill 112, but could advance no further. The entire 129 Brigade came under heavy attack, with ferocious assaults directed against the Somerset Light Infantry. To strengthen this sector, infantry of the DCLI, supported by tanks, moved through the Somersets towards a wood on the far side of the hill, to clash head on with advancing Tigers with grenadier escorts. Savage fighting ensued in which all the DCLI anti-tank guns were knocked out, some while engaging the Tigers point-blank. The huge tanks depressed their guns and butchered the British infantry in their trenches. Angered, British soldiers refused the surrender of the crew of a knocked-out Tiger, whom they shot down. Another smoke screen was put down but the Tigers charged through it. They caught the British infantry climbing in to transport sent to rescue them and after destroying two escorting tanks the Tigers opened up on the helpless infantry. An order then came for the German tanks to withdraw and the British pushed forward once more to dig in on the reverse slope of Hill 112 in darkness. By then the 43 Division had all its three infantry brigades, and much of its armour, deployed along the ridge from the hill to Eterville. Nearby a brigade of the Canadian 3 Division had crossed the Odon in to the bridge-head.

The battle for the hill continued for days and nights. The massed guns of both sides rarely let up and often only a heavily armoured tank could move there. Almost always Allied aircraft were wheeling and diving, bombing, rocketing and machine-gunning. British soldiers who seized the hilltop by night on 12 July were driven off by Tigers next day. Such was the ferocity of the answering British artillery that by 15 July only the great panzers could still survive there. Before dawn on the sixteenth German grenadiers struggled back to re-occupy their old positions, in a wood now a graveyard of jagged tree stumps. The whole area was cratered by shell holes so close as to overlap. In the first 36 hours fighting alone the British had lost 2,000 men and the Germans almost as many.

The British had succeeded in embroiling, and holding in the battle, the 10 SS Panzer Division, part of the 1 SS Panzer Division, and the 102 SS Heavy Tank Battalion. Panzer Group West had ordered that Hill 112 must under no circumstances be surrendered and the British soldiers had similar orders. Private Laurence Woolard, of Bowburn, Co Durham, attached to the Welsh Regiment, was one of them. Four companies stood constantly on guard over the vital OP on the hill top, deployed in diamond formations and each day moved around in an anti-clockwise direction to take it in turns to be the forward company. 'That guaranteed you coming under a box barrage every four days,' recalls Woolard. 'I've seen 250 men go up to the top and a handful come down. We went up so far on the back of tanks then ran. When we came back we were always mortared.' So that he could dig himself a trench more quickly Woolard once deliberately chose a patch of soft earth that was obviously a recent grave. 'I dug out a German,' he recalls. 'But it was the quickest way below ground.'

The soldiers clinging to Hill 112 were also subjected to constant vicious snipers' fire, so that their days and nights were spent below ground in slit trenches, one man always alert to sounds that might indicate a German attack. Food was delivered by racing Bren carriers and flung in to each trench, perhaps a tin of rice, or steak, always cold.

'Once I was in a trench with a corporal,' remembers Woolard. 'I had just finished my two hours' watch near dawn and gave him a nudge. He was half asleep and put his head just over the top. A sniper put a burst right across his face and his nose and mouth just shot all over me. I had bloody clothes on for a full week afterwards. I saw where the tracer bullets came from, and let go with a Thompson sub-machine-gun. Nothing fell from the outline of the tree. It was checked out and a sniper had fastened himself to a branch so that he could use both hands. He was dead.

'During the night you could hear Jerry crawling through your lines, so you let him go through, but not back. Any night reccc was a suicide trip. You only hoped you weren't to be told you were a volunteer. Our company got caught on the hill in a battle between Jerry tanks and our 17lb and 25lb guns. The shells screamed over about three foot above the trenches.'

By 18 July the last battle for Caen itself had been fought and won and more British infantry were pressing forward around the hill. The streets of Maltot, and fields around, were strewn with the corpses of Dorsets and Hampshires who had fallen there. On Hill 112 shell-scarred Tigers, their armour too thick for penetration, still dominated, however heavily their supporting infantry suffered under the merciless British artillery bombardment.

8 A Galloping 'Goodwood'

There was now an air of mounting urgency about the whole Normandy operation because there were not likely to be more than another six weeks' good campaigning weather. The Allied air forces could be grounded and the Channel too rough. In possession of no more than a fifth of the territory they should have occupied by mid-July, the Allies were finding it increasingly difficult to deploy newly arrived divisions. The only facet that had gone exactly according to plan was the drawing in of the bulk of the enemy armour against the British and Canadians. But if the Americans did not soon take advantage of this bloody self-sacrifice, then the invasion might well be doomed. The ferocity of the head-on Anglo-Canadian onslaught had finally decided Hitler and his High Command that, as the V1 bombardment had failed either to produce a plea for mercy or a furious major assault upon the Pas de Calais, then Normandy *must* be a main Allied effort. So four experienced German infantry divisions from the Fifteenth Army were moved to Normandy, three against the British and Canadians. Geyr von Schweppenburg was to drive an armoured wedge between the British and Americans and then destroy their armies separately. Because the Germans still considered the Americans easy meat by comparison it was decided to defeat them first. To prevent the panzers attacking the Americans Montgomery knew there would have to be yet another British-Canadian sacrifice. Hurriedly he implemented a further offensive, Operation 'Goodwood'.

Intelligence reports had revealed that time was desperately short. Montgomery had to act swiftly, without his usual meticulous planning. An overriding factor was that the British and Canadians were by now very short of infantry who inevitably

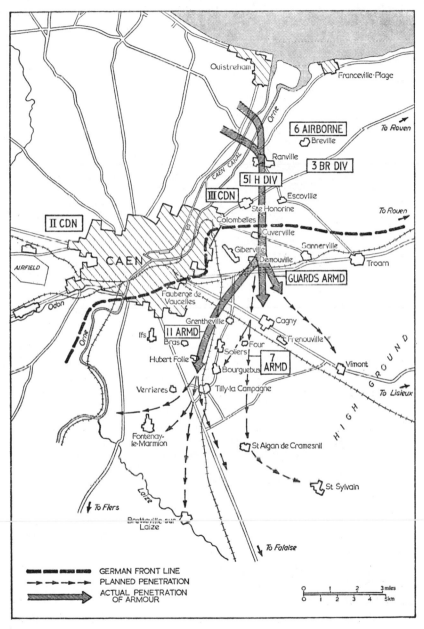

Map 4 'Goodwood' 16–20 July

had suffered very heavy casualties. Even though German losses by now amounted to over 100,000 men, for every German infantryman killed three British and Canadian infantrymen had died. When two armies are equally well armed, the attacking one will always suffer more casualties against an enemy fighting in fortified positions. In addition, the great majority of British and Canadians were experiencing battle for the first time whereas most Germans were veterans of earlier bitter campaigns.

Among British infantry reinforcements now were soldiers of the Royal Artillery, including anti-aircraft gunners, who were given a sketchy six weeks' instruction before being sent to Normandy. Also weighing cruelly against the British and Canadian infantry was the fact that they had trained for so long for a *blitzkrieg* assault on Fortress Europe, but the whole concept of *blitzkrieg* had foundered in the Normandy *bocage*. 'When the Canadian 2 Division needed reinforcements I recall sitting in a field taking down our 3 Division patches and sewing on those of the illustrious Calgary Highlanders,' recalls Edward Ford, of Montreal, originally with the Winnipeg Rifles. 'Those were the days of 12-men platoons and feverish digging of slit trenches, when you saw the sun set and wondered if you would live to see it rise . . .'

Because of his shortage of infantry, Montgomery had to plan 'Goodwood' around an opening head-on assault by massed tanks, a sort of Charge of the Light Brigade on to the strongly fortified enemy positions and into the inevitable high velocity barrage of the 88mm guns. Not only could wrecked tanks be replaced readily but often the majority of the crews escaped to be back in action in replacements. (On average 1·5 men per crew became casualties, not necessarily fatal, when a tank was 'brewed up'.) There was a reserve of over 500 tanks in Normandy and two more fully trained armoured divisions—the 4 Canadians and 1 Polish—were near the coast in England ready to enter the battle.

Unfortunately nowhere in the terrain so far won by the Twenty-first Army Group was there ground suitable for a massed tank assault. Montgomery decided to launch one from the constricted bridge-head originally won by the airborne troops east of the Orne. It was overlooked by the enemy established on the high ground of the Bois de Bavent and the factory suburb of Colombelles due east of Caen. In addition the ground would bottleneck the tanks into a line of advance only a few tanks wide. The great charge of the massed armour would have to be made virtually line ahead instead of the required line abreast, under the guns of the enemy until they had penetrated south of Caen to territory suitable for wider deployment. Instead of infantry making the initial breaches as was customary, the necessary gaps were to be blasted by a massive bombing raid.

The great tank attack, to go in on 18 July, was to be headed by the 11 Armoured Division commanded by the very experienced Major General G. P. B. (Pip) Roberts. On its heels were to go the Guards Armoured Division, relative newcomers to warfare, with the 7 Armoured Division swiftly to exploit any breakthrough. Inevitably as this thin arm of armour thrust out into enemy territory it must be subjected to close-range artillery fire and powerful panzer counter-attack. Throughout its projected six miles advance to the high ground around the main Caen–Falaise road, the armour would be suicidally close to a parallel line of linked, strongly fortified villages to the south. On their northern flank they would be equally lethally close to the powerfully fortified factory area of Colombelles, Mondeville and Cormelles. Once beyond, the armoured divisions were to strike out for separate objectives: 11 Armoured to Fontenay le Marmion and Bretteville-sur-Laize and southwards towards Falaise; 7 Armoured towards the Falaise road and St Aignan de Cramesnil and onwards to St Sylvain; and the Guards through Cagny onward to the same area and south-eastwards to Vimont. The advance must cross two railway embankments and seize the commanding high ground between the two national highways, the N13 Paris road and N158 Falaise road. In the armour's wake British infantry were to clear up the enemy strongpoints on the left and Canadian infantry those on the right.

The territorial restrictions upon the initial deployment of the tanks also denied them a sufficient artillery support. There just was not room enough for the guns required to bombard the formidable German defences. Thus when the armoured divisions had advanced no further than half way, they would be beyond the range of the massed 25-pounders and almost suicidally vulnerable to the flanking enemy guns. Weather permitting, however, they would have the spectacular support of the rocket-firing Typhoons. Already British tank men had observed, with approval, how the crews of even Tiger tanks would bail out in panic when subjected to the terrifying rockets fired in these low-level attacks. It particularly pleased the veteran Desert Rats who still remembered the days when Rommel's more powerful armoured columns, with supporting Stuka dive-bombers, dominated North Africa. The Typhoons liaised closely in what was known as a 'cab rank'. There was a radio link between a leading tank commander and the RAF fighter-bombers which circled the battlefield ready to blast any target indicated. The system worked spectacularly—unless the control tank was knocked out.

To challenge the Typhoons the enemy had very little. Despite Hitler's order that 'anti-aircraft highways' should be created by the Luftwaffe, so that men and vehicles could move protected by ranging fighters, the Focke-Wulfs and the Messerschmitts just did not materialise. Although nearly all the 800 single-engined fighters defending Germany had been switched to Normandy, they at no time offered any serious opposition. Nearly half the Luftwaffe fighters had been destroyed and their airfields so devastated that few could take to the air. In the past three months the German factories had delivered no less than a record 4,545 single-engined fighters. During the same period, 5,527 were shot down, or destroyed on the ground. Meanwhile the heavy bombers of the RAF and USAAF had resumed their day and night bombardment of German home industry, and in June oil production fell from the 175,000 tons of April to a mere 53,000 tons. This was cause for recall to the Reich of eight groups of fighters leaving Allied planes to roam the battlefield virtually unopposed.

Intelligence reports suggested that the German defences

ended somewhere about the line of the Caen–Vimont railway. After that the tanks should be able to race on at will a further four miles to seize the vital Bourguébus Ridge. Once there it was not likely they would have to face enemy armoured counter-attack in any sort of strength. It was believed that the 21 Panzer Division was inextricably committed to positions in Vaucelles and the only panzers in reserve were what remained of the 12 SS Panzer Division. In fact, the German High Command had ordered that newly arrived infantry divisions should relieve the armour committed to the British-Canadian front by 1 August. Three armoured corps, comprising seven panzer divisions, were to make a massive attack deep into the British rear around Caen. Any threat of an American break-out in the west was still considered of no consequence.

Montgomery planned to use the Allies' available air power in an unprecedented manner. The German defences were to be obliterated by the greatest air armada ever sent against an enemy army. There would be 2,000 bombers, 2,000 fighter-bombers and 720 guns. No enemy should survive such a holocaust, unleashed upon them even before the charge of the three armoured divisions, expected to race through a desolation of shattered defences to seize the vital Bourguébus Ridge. Even if it cost 300 tanks the great armoured charge must be worth it because the key to the Normandy battlefield would be in British hands. Beyond was the splendid tank country of the Normandy plains and the fine road to Falaise, dead straight for 16 miles, ideal for a triumphant onrush. As soon as 'Goodwood' had been launched, Bradley's US First Army would make its assault. When the American offensive, Operation 'Cobra', was launched two days later, to and through St Lô, the armies of the Allies would wheel eastwards together to sweep forward in triumphant attack. Laval–Mayenne and Le Mans–Alençon were successive objectives Montgomery named as immediate goals for Patton's armour.

Montgomery was aware that the Americans would not be ready until 25 July. Bradley had ordered Major-General T. H. Middleton's VIII Corps to advance to Coutances but the enemy defence had been bitter. Little real progress had been made even though the Americans had sustained heavy casualties. Before the Americans launched 'Cobra' the British and Canadian infantry would mop up the enemy defence positions through which the armoured divisions had charged. In Montgomery's planning Caen had always been the hinge on which the Americans would pivot to switch their drive from southwards to eastwards, a solid hinge against which no enemy attack could succeed. The British would again deliberately draw all German armour against them while the Americans finally burst clear of the lethal restrictions of the Normandy battlefield to go racing away in the enemy's rear. But Eisenhower appeared to misunderstand because he spoke of Bradley keeping his troops 'fighting like the very devil . . . to provide the opportunity your armoured corps will need . . .'

When Montgomery meanwhile sent his Military Assistant (Lieut Colonel C. Dawnay) to explain his intentions to the War Office, he emphasised that '[Montgomery] is aiming at doing the greatest damage to enemy armour, Caen–Falaise is the only place this can be done . . . All the activities on the eastern flank are designed to help the American forces.' What Montgomery was now setting out to do was deliberately to attack the very place where the Germans had concentrated their maximum strength in greatest depth. At whatever cost to his British and Canadian troops, he intended to compel the enemy so totally to commit their armoured divisions, that they would have nothing left with which to challenge the Americans when George Patton's tank army finally went racing away.

The terrible battle of attrition at Caen had compelled the Germans to squander their counter-attacking strength. It was not anticipated that they would be able to put up much of a fight after they had been subjected to the opening 'Goodwood' bombardment. The strongpoint village of Cagny alone was to be hit by a sudden earthquake of 650 tons of RAF bombs! Meanwhile the fortified chain of 45 villages on the left flank were to be pulverised by 2,500 tons of bombs and the equally heavily fortified Caen-Mondeville industrial district on the right was to be hit with a simultaneous 2,500 tons. A USAAF bomber armada was to saturate all the central strongpoints directly in the path of the advancing armoured divisions with anti-personnel bombs to kill men (rather than high explosive that would tear up the ground). After the massive bombing of Caen, ruins had held up the British advance. Another mistake now to be rectified was that the ground attack would go in *immediately* behind the air onslaught when surviving Germans should be incapable of resisting. This was to be the greatest battlefield air-raid in the history of warfare.

The armoured divisions had stealthily crept up to their assembly areas where it had become apparent that the confined nature of the bridge-head through which they must advance would present many difficulties. Not the least was a minefield laid earlier by a British division, now squarely in their path. Because it was hoped secrecy could be maintained, the best that could be done was the lifting of sufficient mines to open up just a few narrow lanes one tank wide. Through these the tanks, guns and infantry half-tracks of three armoured divisions would have to flow to be followed by the self-propelled guns of the divisional artillery and all the fuel tankers, ammunition trucks and supply wagons necessary. They were committed to an advance through a zone of strongly fortified defences that extended for ten miles, not just the three or four miles believed to be their maximum depth. Rommel was determined to prevent a British break-out.

The Germans had made their minds up there would be a big attack. Reconnaissance aircraft had reported a vast movement of British armour, and German agents among the Normandy population had reported an impending big attack. To make his plans Rommel held a conference with General Wilhelm Bittrich, commander of the II SS Panzer Corps and General 'Sepp' Dietrich, commanding I SS Panzer Corps. To challenge the three armoured divisions and seven armoured brigades the British were throwing into the attack, the Germans were employing six armoured divisions and three heavy tank battalions. While the British formations had been kept at full strength, however, the German divisions were mostly depleted. Only the newly arrived 1 SS Panzer Division and four new German infantry divisions had their full complement of men and machines.

But the Germans were deployed in depth in well prepared positions, protected by extensive minefields and formidably covered by many of the high velocity 88mm guns and the multi-barrelled mortars of three Nebelwerfer brigades. The scores of Norman villages incorporated in the defences were mostly stone-built and surrounded by orchards, amid thick hedges deeply rooted in massive banks of earth. This, the strongest part of the enemy line, was a formidable sector to attack head-on. Rommel had established five belts of defences east of the Orne. The first was 'expendable' infantry around Vaucelles and north of the first railway embankment, the second was the 21 Panzers reinforced by thirty-six Tigers and a medium panzer battalion of the 1 SS. The third, bestriding the Caen–Vimont railway, was a zone of 12 fortified villages manned by infantry with anti-tank guns. The fourth was a formidable line of artillery along the Bourguébus Ridge stretching as far as the Secqueville woods and then swinging north-east across the railway up to Troarn. There were no less than seventy-eight 88mms in this gun line and twenty-two other heavy flak guns, all sited to deal with tanks. In addition there were 194 field guns and 272 multi-barrelled *nebelwerfers*. Beyond was a fifth defensive zone of fortified villages behind the crest of the ridge, while five miles further back strong armoured groups of the 1 and 12 SS lurked ready to counter-attack. With such a deep defensive array Rommel could well await with confidence the expected British onslaught.

After his conference Rommel hurried away to the Army Group HQ at La Roche-Guyon, driven as usual in his staff Mercedes. Because of the many burning and burned-out vehicles (victims of the RAF) they passed, Rommel's driver diverted along side roads lined with trees. But there were eight Typhoons menacingly circling where the Mercedes emerged once more on to the main road. Two dropped within a few yards of the road and roared along it menacingly after the now racing car. The leading Typhoon opened up with cannon and machine-gun fire which tore into the Mercedes. The driver, fatally hit, lost control. Rommel, two other officers and a bodyguard sergeant were all wounded. The car overturned. An

Plate 15. A British soldier assists an old woman survivor of the bombing of Caen amidst the wilderness of ruins to which the Norman city was reduced

Plate 16. Inevitably thousands of French civilians caught up in the Normandy battle were killed or injured. Equally inevitably when British Tommies had the opportunity to fraternize with survivors, they tried to teach the French cricket. Here a happy British corporal relishes going through the motions with a French girl, though he seems more interested in exploring bodyline theories than teaching her how to play a straight bat

Plate 17. General Patton, complete with pearl-handled six-shooter, and Monty, here seen with Omar Bradley, appear to be enjoying each other's company, even though Patton was highly critical of the British commander

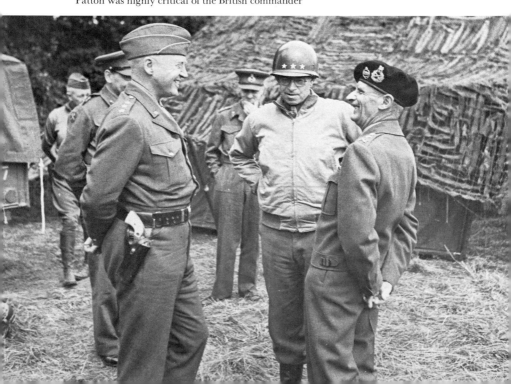

ambulance took the apparently fatally wounded Rommel to hospital. Although he did recover, he was to play no further part in this or any other battle. Hitler was to compel him to take his own life for being implicated in the unsuccessful plot against Hitler's life.

9 The Charge of the Armoured Brigades

At 5.30am on 18 July the obliteration of the German defences began with a bombardment by 720 guns, followed by 1,000 four-engined Lancasters and Halifaxes bombing target areas indicated by the flares dropped by Pathfinders. Their 500lb and 1,000lb bombs were aimed at two long narrow rectangles flanking the route to be followed by the armoured divisions. On the right flank (where the Canadian 3 Infantry Division with the Canadian 2 Infantry Division backing them were to mop up whatever Germans survived) the target area was held by formations of the 21 Panzer Division, well supplied with the deadly 88mm guns. On the left, where the British 3 Infantry Division was due to mop up, the network of heavily fortified villages was manned by the Battle Group Luck, Tiger tanks of the 503 Heavy Tank Battalion and a strong group of the 200 Assault Gun Battalion. After the attackers had run this formidable gauntlet to the left and right, they would be confronted by the 22 Panzer Regiment and the best part of a battalion of Tigers at the end of the bombed area.

The tanks were the principal bombing targets. Sensing this, the crews battened down their hatches and crouched within the iron hulls as the bombers neared them. In the hour-long cataclysm which engulfed them, tanks were burst asunder and others—even the huge Tigers—were blown upside down. Some were hurled many yards, others were completely buried.

John Richardson, of Rainham, Kent, was a Lancaster pilot:

'Cagny was attacked with the Lancasters bombing at only 2,500 feet and the blast from the bombs could be felt in the aircraft. The attack was led by Squadron Leader Alan Craig, DSO, DFC, who marked the target and directed the raid. I can still hear him calling, "Come down. It's lovely down here." And they came down, emerging one by one. What a sight! And what trust the pilots must have put in him. They bombed the markers and I remember seeing a tower with a machine-gun giving everyone hell, and a lone Typhoon looming up and cutting the tower in half with its cannons. What a shot!'

Time and again the Pathfinders came in with new flares to keep the bombers right up on their targets and time and again gigantic eruptions of smoke and flames soared up from the target areas. When it was all over, and the surviving Germans emerged from tanks and dugouts, it was to find that the little villages and farmsteads around them had vanished utterly. So had the trees, the hedges, the ponds and the very fields themselves. They were now in the midst of such an utter desolation that some men called it *mondlandschaft*—moon landscape. And then came the heavy daylight bombers of the USAAF, in apparently endless formations, at a greater height. They ravaged Bras, Grentheville, Hubert Folie and Soliers, grouped beyond the Caen–Vimont railway embankment. The vital heights of Bourguébus, dominating the whole battlefield, were a major target. Another was a rectangle of territory near Troarn, almost due east of Caen. Unfortunately the big American bombers, carrying smaller loads, failed to subject Bourguébus to the intended concentration. And when the American medium bombers followed up with showers of anti-personnel bombs along the actual avenue of advance, they were frequently off target. Their widespread scattering of the small bombs, instead of concentrating them on enemy positions, only served to emphasise that a British offensive was imminent. Bomb aiming had been difficult in the vast pall of smoke and dust already raised.

But at Demouville the American medium bombers achieved outstanding success. One whole assault-gun battalion and a battalion of Panzer Grenadiers were decimated. Practically all the infantry of the 716 Luftwaffe Field Division were killed, wounded or shocked into a state of non-resistance. Tanks that had to be dug out in many cases had engines and cooling systems choked with earth and instruments out of alignment. Many surviving crews were so shaken as to be unfit for action. But back on the dominating Bourguébus Ridge, a deadly menace to the British attack, were lined up the seventy-eight terrible 88mm guns. Somehow the American heavy bombers had missed them.

Von Kluge, now in command, reported to Hitler: 'In face of the enemy's complete command of the air, there is no possibility of our finding a strategy which will counter-balance its truly annihilating effect . . . The psychological effect of such a mass of bombs coming down with all the power of elemental nature upon the fighting troops, especially infantry, is a factor which has to be given particularly serious consideration.' And von Kluge added the warning: 'The moment has drawn near when this front, already so heavily strained, will break.' But Hitler merely reiterated his order to stand fast.

As the British guns had leaped into life, projecting a thunderous barrage ahead of the advancing armour, tanks of the 3 Royal Tank Regiment rumbled forward in single file through the minefield. On the far side, where they could deploy to some extent, they formed into waves of 32 tanks to a line. Flail tanks, to deal with enemy minefields, engineer tanks to remove obstacles, motorised infantry and self-propelled guns, formed up in successive waves. Then, after the holocaust of the bombers, behind the thunderous artillery barrage, they moved forward. In view of the shattering bombing, viewed with an awed approval by the waiting troops, most men did not expect much opposition. They hoped for an easy ride to a notable victory. The tanks of the Fife and Forfar Yeomanry followed those of the 3 Royal Tank Regiment, then came the 23 Hussars. As they plunged into the dust and smoke they began to lose formation, to be slowed by having to drive around vast bomb craters. Soon they were not maintaining the planned pace just behind the protective curtain of high explosives the guns were putting down. Where there should have been 100 yards between the waves, there was soon in some cases a full mile. The iron fist being driven at the shaken Germans was already unclenching.

Dr Ron Cox, of Sanderstead, Surrey, a Lance Corporal in

the 2 Fife and Forfar Yeomanry, remembers how 18 July had dawned warm and sunny. They were aware 'something was afoot' because during the previous night they had been ordered to drive from the area west of Caen to the village of Ranville:

'We heard the drone of bombers which passed over our heads and a short distance in front of us dropped their loads. It seemed that whatever hidden opposition had been in front of us must have been totally obliterated. As the bombing ceased the sun came out and we began to advance. From then on my view was through the tank periscope. We moved forward for some distance behind a creeping barrage, then we stopped. I remember opening a new tin of jam and spreading it thickly on innumerable biscuits and passing them round to the crew. We exchanged banter: I think the humour was a bit forced and had a slight hysterical touch to it for we were all aware that this was going to be something rather big. We couldn't possibly have foreseen that we were about to play a part in the last large-scale set tank-battle that the world is ever likely to see. My own emotion was a kind of numbed fatalism.'

But for the tanks leading the great armoured drive things were going fairly well. As the 3 RTR pressed on into ravaged wheatfields they were virtually untroubled by the fortified villages of Cuverville and Demouville on their right because the bombs had obliterated both men and guns. And from the wheat trembling German infantrymen, ashen faces proclaiming the bombing's effect, arose with arms raised. Others, still slumped in foxholes and slit trenches, seemed too dazed even to stand up. The leading British tanks rumbled on to cross the first railway embankment, the Caen–Troarn line, and by now the first waves of the 3 RTR and the Fife and Forfar Yeomanry were in line abreast. They were nearing the closely grouped villages of Manneville, Cuverville and Emieville where German Tiger and Mark IV tanks were lying in wait. The advancing British tank crews were soon aware of their presence and the commanders would have liked to have attacked to clear the villages, but orders were to press on.

Although the villages had been deluged with fragmentation

bombs, by some mischance the section of each village that faced on to the line of the British advance had escaped. The German soldiers were still mostly prepared to fight to the death rather than surrender. The advancing tanks were still under the protection of the British artillery but would be beyond its furthest range when they crossed the Caen–Vimont railway embankment. Before they reached the railway, however, they must encounter the fortified village of Cagny, the point at which the three armoured divisions were to strike out in different directions. The 11 Armoured were to go straight on to attack Bourguébus, the Guards were to swing left and drive for Vimont and the 7 Armoured when past Cagny were to fan out between the concentrated thrusts of the other two divisions. Their main objective was the concentration of German guns around Secqueville but they were to be ready to move to the aid of 11 Armoured or Guards Armoured as events might require.

It was from Cagny that each of the three armoured thrusts would spring out in different directions, so this had to be territory not subjected to enemy fire. A major assumption in the British plan was that Cagny's defences would be obliterated by the RAF bombing. Moreover, a very basic assumption about the defences of Cagny, based on faulty intelligence reports, was that it was garrisoned by infantry. In fact, it was held by no less than the powerful Battle Group Luck, comprising the 125 Panzer Grenadiers, part of the 22 Panzer Regiment, the Tigers of 503 Heavy Tank Battalion and the formidable guns of the 200 Assault Gun Battalion. The garrison of Cagny was a tank-killing force par excellence. It could destroy the attackers long before their guns could range on the Cagny defences. And those defences, against all predictions, had suffered comparatively little damage from the massive RAF bombing. Oberst Freiherr Hans von Luck, Commander of the Battle Group which bore his name, had been on short leave in Paris and did not arrive until after the bombing. He learned that the 1 Battalion of the 125 Panzer Grenadier Regiment, part of his available force, had been virtually obliterated. What remained had already been steamrollered by the onrushing tide of British armour.

Even at that moment a compact mass of some fifty tanks of the Fife and Forfar Yeomanry and the 3 Royal Tank Regiment were crossing the Caen–Vimont railway embankment. Von Luck was ignorant of the fact that the crack 1 SS Panzer Division was ready to counter-attack from the Falaise road behind the Bourguébus Ridge, in the very nick of time relieved from their defensive deployment by a newly arrived infantry division. He presumed his Battle Group was the last barrier capable of stemming the British onrush. He was convinced that he could halt the whole advance by blasting the leading wave of tanks even now about to display their lightly armoured sides to his 88mm guns. But he found the battery commander reluctant to engage. Von Luck drew his revolver and threatened the officer. He obeyed. The guns hurled their huge shells with deadly accuracy at the British tanks. A dozen Shermans burst into ugly pyres of boiling black smoke and red flame. The 23 Hussars, in the following wave, ground to a halt as they came up towards the line of burning Shermans. Nevertheless, Mark IV tanks of the 21 Panzer Division, which had survived the bombing, were roughly handled when sent in to counter-attack. Very few returned. The Tigers of the 503 Heavy Tank Battalion, however, caused widespread destruction amongst the ranks of the 23 Hussars.

As the 3 RTR roared on they were heavily hit by anti-tank guns in Le Mesnil Frementel. The enemy defences here included many heavy-calibre anti-tank guns including 105mm, 88mm and 75mm, some of them multi-barrelled, which had also escaped the aerial bombardment. Going all out for Bourguébus Ridge, the 3 RTR streamed by along both sides of these formidable fortified gun positions and suffered heavily. Although the British tanks rolled right over some multi-barrelled mortars in open cornfields, they could do little against the dug-down heavy anti-tank guns. Soon the battlefield was littered with blazing tanks, yet they continued to advance in successive waves giving each other covering fire. Despite all the blazing wrecks and limping survivors in their wake, the 3 RTR maintained its progress towards the ridge-top villages of Bras and Hubert Folie, some 3,000 yards ahead across open terrain.

They seemed to have penetrated the last line of enemy defences. Now the 3 RTR and Fife and Forfar Yeomanry roared up the slope in mass formation to overrun their final objective.

'At first we seemed to advance quite rapidly,' recalls Ron Cox. 'Then, suddenly, my tank ground to a halt, as did all the others I could see. The Tigers and anti-tank gunners on our flanks had apparently let the 3 Tanks pass through and had then opened up on the Fife and Forfar Yeomanry. The worst fire, from anti-tank batteries in Cagny, fell particularly on my squadron. The first tank hit was that of Major Nicholls, our Squadron Leader. So was that of his second-in-command, Capt Miller . . . Other tanks I could see were all stationary and several were beginning to brew. Dust and smoke were combining with the heat-haze to make visibility more and more difficult. I had nothing to do. There were no targets. Nothing intelligible was coming over the radio. I watched through the periscope, fascinated, as though it was a film I was seeing.

'Then over the intercom came the totally unruffled voice of Sergeant Wally Herd: "Driver reverse . . . driver halt . . ." I remember thinking "Good old Wally, he's getting us out." On reflection though, he can't have rated our chances high. There was absolutely no cover and furthermore our tank was the one per troop that had been converted to a Firefly— that is, its 75mm gun had been replaced with a 17-pounder, making it in silhouette a much more conspicuous and attractive target. Then suddenly there was a tremendous crash and shudder. We had been hit. It was a glancing blow but the track was broken. The next shot would follow as soon as the enemy gun could be reloaded. Wally Herd shouted "Bale out!" As we baled out and ran, crouched down, away from the tank, it was hit a second time and smoke began to pour from it.'

When the stricken Yeomanry went off the air, having lost 57 of their 61 tanks, the Hussars were sent forward. They realised just what had happened to their predecessors when they entered a wilderness of burning Yeomanry tanks. Then the enemy guns were directed upon the Hussars: everywhere their tanks flamed in this awful graveyard of British armour. The great Charge of the Armoured Brigades that had set out with such high hopes had ended with the path of their advance strewn with 106 knocked-out tanks. Guards Armoured had also suffered heavily, losing 60 tanks before grinding to a halt west of Cagny. When they turned away south-east towards Vimont they were subjected to a ferocious flanking fire from both Cagny and Emieville. Though they pressed on regardless, they were finally halted by a formidable line of guns and tanks well dug-down in orchards east of Frenouville.

The 7 Armoured, which in the initial congestion had not yet even fully cleared the first minefield, were sustaining casualties from enemy guns which had inexplicably survived the bombing. They had only one armoured regiment in action beyond the Caen–Vimont railway by nightfall. What befell 7 Armoured is remembered by Robert Boulton:

'It was even worse than the *bocage*. All I remember of "Goodwood" is sitting for most of one night in a traffic jam waiting to cross a bridge and the non-existent Luftwaffe being very existent. When we did get across tanks and trucks were on fire all over the place. The dust was absolutely choking.

'Our section pulled off the road just opposite the dressing stations of the 1/6 Queen's, who were doing an attack. A long and continuous stream of casualties were coming in. I remember saying there would be nothing left of the 1/6 if this went on much longer. Worse still, there was a poor lad who had had most of the bottom of his back blown away. There was nothing to be done for him so he was just put outside on a stretcher. That poor devil screamed for about two hours; morphine seemed to have no effect. He was pleading for someone to finish him off. Our sergeant had been in the war from the start, and even he was white and shaken.'

The Guards valiantly resumed their battle for Cagny until they were well into the ruined village. The Irish Guards of the division meanwhile fought a bitter close-quarters battle with 21 Panzer Division before finally securing a footing on the ridge to the east. The Germans at Cagny were not overcome until British infantry were brought up. They found the whole area an inferno, to which dozens of knocked-out British tanks added their flames and smoke. 'Our tanks were sitting ducks and were soon reduced to burning wrecks,' remembers Harold Watling, of Bromley, Kent, a private in 128 Field Ambulance, attached to the Guards Armoured Division.

Watling recalls an act of outstanding self-sacrifice by an Irish Guardsman during the attack. The Germans were firing incendiary bullets into a cornfield where many wounded lay. Suddenly the Guardsman stood erect firing his Bren gun to draw the enemy fire while some wounded were dragged clear. He fell, riddled with bullets. When German wounded were brought in Watling removed a bandage from an officer, who became very agitated, and found that he had no wound. The officer had pretended he was wounded because he feared he would be shot otherwise. In the dressing stations there was a noticeable change now in the type of casualties. Richard Read of Sawbridgeworth, Herts, an RASC Lance Corporal attached to 32 FDS, recalls: 'Previously our surgeons had found mainly gunshot wounds and the result of being blown up by the hundreds of mines put down. The pattern changed and the wounded were mainly tank crews burnt so badly that in many cases their clothes were burned to their bodies.'

The delay in taking Cagny had given the Germans time to bring up the 12 SS behind Bourguébus. Yet another attempt was made to overrun the ridge, this time by the 2 Northants Yeomanry. They met a fate similar to all the others under the fire of the line of dug-down 88mm guns. As darkness fell the 1 SS Panzers, who had been south of the bombed area, sent in a counter-attack. The 11 Armoured Division, who during this day of fury had lost 126 tanks, more than half their strength, were compelled to draw back to a line north of the Caen–Vimont railway for the night. And back along the whole line of the British advance, littered as it was with wrecked tanks and troop-carrying vehicles, a growing confusion developed.

Into it enemy long-range artillery directed a damaging fire. Meanwhile south of the Caen–Vimont railway the Germans still held all the fortified villages but one, and on the Bourguébus Ridge they were drawn up in powerful array.

On this night the Luftwaffe sent in an unusually strong force which attacked the rear echelons. In such a congested area they could not miss and caused serious casualties among surviving crews from knocked out tanks and replacement crews. 'A German anti-personnel bomb blew its splinters, forwards and sideways, about one inch from the ground,' recalls Colin Thomson. 'From that moment it was standing orders that everyone slept below ground. It was a fearful sensation hearing the bombs coming down whining and screaming towards your shallow foxhole, which seemed dreadfully exposed and inadequate.'

10 The Canadian Armageddon

To the left of the bloody charge of the armoured brigades the British 3 Infantry Division, with a brigade of the 51 Division and supported by 27 Armoured Brigade, had swept through Sannerville and Banneville la Campagne, whose bomb-stupefied defenders offered little resistance. But they were drawn into heavy fighting at Touffreville, which had escaped the heaviest bombing, and along the road to Troarn amongst enemy minefields in broken country south of Bavent Wood. By midnight however the villages of Banneville and Guillerville had been taken and only Troarn and Emieville remained in enemy hands. When the British infantry tried to storm Emieville, they were halted by the same heavily armed force that had savaged the Guards.

The Canadians early encountered trouble in the factory area of Colombelles and Vaucelles. The German guns which had survived, and there were many of them, made maximum use of the cover provided by the wrecked factories and other buildings. The planned sweep south by the Canadian 3 Division on the Orne's east bank was seriously delayed. So was the complementary attack by one brigade from the middle of ruined Caen across the Orne into Vaucelles. But by nightfall the Canadians, guided by a member of the French Resistance, had streamed across the river to enter this suburb. Surviving Germans contrived to pull out in the darkness to reinforce the western end of the Bourguébus Ridge. The Canadian casualties that day were 1,500 men and 200 tanks. They had also brought the industrial suburbs of Caen within the British front so that the whole city was now securely held.

Despite the undeniable petering out of the great British 'Goodwood' offensive, Montgomery that night issued a special announcement for the BBC which stated that the Second Army had broken through. 'Operations this morning a complete success,' he informed the CIGS. 'The effect of the air bombing was decisive and the spectacle terrific.' He went on to state that the 11 Armoured Division had reached Tilly la Campagne and Bras, that the Guards had passed Cagny and were in Vimont and that 7 Armoured were moving on La Hogue. None of these objectives had been attained even though earlier it might have seemed probable. 'Situation very promising and it is difficult to see what the enemy can do just at present,' Montgomery had ended his message. But British and Canadian troops were already finding out!

There was indeed every indication that Montgomery had done it again. Even Dempsey, in closer touch with the fighting, had declined an offer by the Second Tactical Air Force to bomb and rocket the enemy behind Bourguébus Ridge because he believed their strength did not merit it. However, strong formations of the 1 SS were brought up during the night to take over from the exhausted 21 Panzers. If the full weight of the bombers had again been used next day on the northern slopes of Bourguébus Ridge, Operation 'Goodwood' might even then have achieved its full objective. But the devastating Allied bombing force was already committed to the coming American offensive.

When the 3 RTR attacked again next day they were at little more than half strength, despite reinforcements. As they approached Bourguébus Ridge, more circumspectly than before, they encountered the heavy fire of both guns and tanks, while German infantry were in strength in the cornfields around Bras. Soon the armoured attack was halted; the enemy were even stronger. It was, however, possible to bring up batteries of British field guns to give their considerable support and, although the Northants Yeomanry suffered heavily when struck in the flank by German artillery in Ifs, 3 RTR made good progress behind a barrage and smoke. Close behind were their shock-troop infantry, the 8 KRRC. By nightfall the 1 SS Panzers had been routed at Bras, leaving the village strewn with their dead and a dozen self-propelled guns. The ferocity of the fighting was such that of the 63 tanks with which they had started 3 RTR had only nine fully serviceable. All troop officers, and all but one troop sergeant, had been killed or wounded. But they had achieved their objective.

Every regiment of 11 Armoured Division that had climbed Bourguébus Ridge had been shattered. But although the charge of the tank brigades had been so costly, it had finally thrust right through to the vital high ground. This, however, did not mean that 'Goodwood' had succeeded. Instead of a formidable armoured force occupying the very thresholds of Falaise, the offensive had pushed a battered remnant of an armoured division up onto Bourguébus Ridge. And by the sultry high noon of 20 July this costly thrust was hemmed in by strong components of the 21 Panzer Division, the 1 SS Panzers and the 12 SS and 272 Infantry Divisions. The full strength 116 Panzer Division, moved across from the Pas de Calais, was meanwhile coming into the line. Even though Dempsey was eager to push on, Montgomery now required the Caen pivot first to be made absolutely impregnable. To his mind the early loss of impetus, and the unexpectedly strong intervention by Battle Group Luck, had retarded the 'Goodwood' offensive so much that it could no longer be effectively maintained. The narrow stream of British armour had not become an unstoppable tide.

Montgomery now wanted to marshal his forces around Caen to create a strong pivot on which his all-out offensive—the American one—would hinge. Afterwards his critics were to attribute this to his 'extreme caution and inflexibility'. The news of the stupendous air bombardment and Montgomery's own use of the words 'break through' had led to a general belief that an important victory had been won. Instead he was pulling back his armour 'to consolidate'. But however disappointing the outcome, about thirty more square miles of Normandy had been cleared of the enemy, heavy casualties had been inflicted, Caen was finally captured, and the bulk of the enemy armour had been committed.

But if Montgomery was being cautious, his German counterpart was equally fallible. Von Kluge, assured the developing British attack was 'an attempt by the enemy to provide himself with a suitable jumping-off position for the offensive expected in two or three days,' had left for his HQ at Poitiers, 200 miles distant, even as 'Goodwood' was launched. His orders were that Panzer Group West must push them right back behind a line from Caen to Troarn. Hitler (who demanded this) still believed the Allies would attempt the second landing. By the day's end von Kluge had realised how serious the British threat was and called up the 12 SS Panzer Division from Lisieux and the 116 Panzer Division from the Seine.

Beneath lowering skies the tanks of 7 Armoured Division moved out on 20 July from beyond Bras and Hubert Folie to let the infantry of the Canadian 2 Division through to attack Verrières Ridge beyond Bourguébus. A delay in the 7 Armoured move gave time for the enemy to reinforce.

'The Calgary Highlanders moved around midnight across country to the western end of the notorious Bourguébus Ridge,' recollects Edward Ford. 'We were greatly encouraged to see the impressive array of Allied armour all around us and at dawn we moved on to Rocquancourt. We were shelled, there was little cover and speedy digging of slit trenches was necessary . . . I recall moving across the dry fields, first in arrowhead then in extended line using aerial photographs. One scene still very vivid in my mind is the battalion pinned down in a war-torn wheat field, pock marked with craters, criss-crossed with tank tracks, the shelling nerve-racking. I shepherded men into shell and bomb craters, spread out as thinly as possible. I can well remember digging into a tank track with my bare hands . . .

'Around us we could see our tanks ablaze. Artillery rounds fell short, comrades fell to right and left . . . Advancing over open country, between long lines of evil-looking woods, the enemy made good use of machine-gun fire and mortars at short range in our left flank. The supporting tanks of the 1 Hussars silenced an 88mm and multi-barrelled *nebelwerfers* raining shells on our forward companies from about 400 yards. Eventually the village was taken after the tanks had succeeded in eliminating a German machine-gun position at the hill top. We were preparing to dig in, providing all-round defence when, much to our dismay, orders came to withdraw to the high ground to the north. Anger filled my mind . . . We had been taught never to get caught moving backwards on a forward slope . . .'

Up on Verrières Ridge were at least 100 tanks of the 1 SS and a Battle Group from 2 Panzers with strong formations of the German 272 Infantry Division. Soldiers of the South Saskatchewan Regiment, with great dash, attained their objective in the centre of the ridge. But before they could consolidate they were cut to pieces by an onrush of German tanks and the survivors scrambled back down the hill. The panzers pursuing them then hit the Essex Scottish and drove them back with heavy losses. Further to the north-east along the ridge, the Fusiliers Mont Royal were similarly overrun by panzers and only a handful came back from the two forward companies. Canadian infantry and gunners fought a brutal battle with the rampaging panzers. Then tanks of the Canadian 2 Armoured Brigade went in to help the Fusiliers Mont Royal assault Beauvois and Toteville Farm and after bitter fighting achieved their objective. Later the Canadian Black Watch, with tanks and artillery support, regained some of the lost ground on the ridge.

The attack was renewed, against ferocious enemy opposition, by the tanks and infantry of the Canadian II Corps, with what was left of the British 7 and Guards Armoured Divisions close behind to exploit any break-through. The slopes up to Verrières Ridge, the dominating height of the whole battlefield, were heavily shelled by the massed guns of the enemy artillery and tanks, multi-barrelled mortars and many machine-guns. The ground was soon strewn with dead and dying Canadian soldiers advancing west and east of the main Falaise–Paris road. The German guns were hidden in strongly fortified positions in the villages beside this road and in surrounding mine galleries and shafts. When the Canadian Black Watch charged through corn raked by machine-guns and devastated by artillery some 60 men reached the ridge top, but only 15 got back. Nearly 350 Canadian infantrymen were killed or wounded.

Plate 17A. British infantrymen cautiously observe through a hedge, knowing that almost certainly German machine guns and mortars are waiting to deluge them with fire the moment they show themselves

Plate 18. From a hastily dug position along a hedge near the crest of Hill 112 British infantry prepare to meet yet another enemy counter attack. Sleep could only be snatched, whenever there was a lull, in the manner of the exhausted soldier in the foxhole in the foreground

Plate 19. The fighting for the high ground that dominated the battlefield south of Caen was bitter. Because of its vital importance the German artillery observers had it pinpointed and here British infantry crouch in a ditch near a ridge as the enemy guns open up

Plate 20. British 'cruiser' tanks advance line ahead, as they were compelled to do out of the constricted Airborne bridgehead in the 'Goodwood' offensive

The Royal Hamilton Light Infantry made a desperate attack on the village of Verrières supported by some 17-pounder anti-tank guns of the 2 Anti-tank Regiment and 16 tanks of the 1 Hussars. On the very threshold of Verrières they dug in and the anti-tank guns knocked out a number of panzers, one gun claiming four. They surged forward again but sustained fearful casualties and every tank was knocked out. When almost up to the village they were only saved from a powerful enemy counter-attack when a devastating barrage was put down by the artillery and mortars. Then Typhoons blasted advancing German tanks and infantry. Dug in just behind the top of the Verrières Ridge, the Canadians were subjected to relentless bombardment. The ground in which they crouched in hastily dug slit trenches seemed in a state of perpetual eruption, the air shrill with shrieking shell splinters. The dead who littered the battlefield, hit again and again, were often blown to pieces. The wounded were rescued only by the bravery and often self-sacrifice of their comrades. It seemed impossible that anything could remain alive on the ridge. The Germans tried to shake the Canadians by sending in their latest secret weapons, miniature radio-controlled tanks packed with 150lb of high explosive. The anti-tank gunners destroyed them.

Tanks from the British 7 Armoured Division somehow got through to Verrières while the German gunners were deluged with mortar fire. They helped bombard enemy strongpoints. Most of the Germans holding Verrières were crack SS Troops, prepared to fight to the death. 'Our feelings towards the enemy I find surprising,' recalls Robert Boulton. 'We felt nearer to them than to civilians. We did not hate the general run of the German army—but the SS were another matter! You didn't think you would survive if taken prisoner by the SS. I do know that some SS did not survive being taken prisoner by the British!'

To the imminence of violent death was now added the discomfort of dysentery, spread among the troops by the swarms of flies which hovered over the battlefield. The stench of the battlefield, littered with decomposing bodies and the rotting carcasses of cattle and horses, was such that just to breath was often to

G

induce a desperate retching. Above all else the men were aching for sleep, something they could only take in perilous snatches in the midst of the constant uproar of battle. In addition, clouds of mosquitoes tormented them as they crouched in their slit trenches. As night closed in on the flaring battlefield, the storm in the heavens finally broke. A deluge of rain soon transformed dust into knee-deep mud. It was all that was needed to end the 'Goodwood' offensive, to bog it down in a sea of mud. 'Goodwood' had most certainly not achieved what Montgomery had said it would, and had been a horrifyingly bloody affair. But the main intention had been, as ever, to draw in the panzer divisions so that Patton's armour could achieve the decisive break-out with minimum opposition. Montgomery ordered that operations on the British front should be continued energetically to keep the enemy's armour committed against them. Meanwhile he was planning a major attack on Falaise for early in August, expecting that the American drive would by then have turned eastwards and be making rapid progress. But on 21 July the Americans had still not gone. The US First Army had become bogged down in the *bocage* and swamps north-west of St Lô, which ruined town they finally took on 19 July. Bradley was being ultra-cautious before he committed himself to the 'Cobra' offensive, which should have been unleashed when the great mass of the German armour was embroiled in 'Goodwood'. But that battle had ended and still the Americans hung back. Because good weather was as vital to 'Cobra' as to 'Goodwood', Bradley was still not prepared to give the word to go, though his 19 superbly armed American divisions were faced by no more than 9 scratch German divisions, with little more than 100 tanks, none of them Tigers.

The 14 divisions of British and Canadians had taken on an equal number of Germans, but mostly crack divisions with 600 tanks including many Tigers. It had been inevitable that losses in men and armour would be terrible on both sides. In the face of their awful casualties the morale of German soldiers was getting low and their commanders tried to hearten them with promises of terrible new secret weapons which would bring sudden victory. 'I have read a fair bit about Normandy and how we "lost our dash" or how the infantry went to ground rather than pressing on,' recalls Colin Thomson. 'Where, I wonder, were the people who wrote this? Do they realise . . . just what the British Army went through?'

11 'One of the Craziest Nights'

Despite all their casualties, the British and Canadians continued to keep the panzers away from the Americans. The Canadian 3 Infantry Division was purposefully thrusting out from Bourguébus towards Tilly la Campagne, which the North Nova Scotia Highlanders succeeded in entering. But the 1 SS Panzer Division counter-attacked fiercely. The Canadian infantry suffered heavy casualties and a supporting tank squadron was decimated. By nightfall their attack had been battered back to Bourguébus. At Verrières the Royal Hamilton Light Infantry held on despite savage German counter-attacks. An attempt by the Royal Regiment of Canada to push on to Rocquancourt was blasted back by a dug-down screen of guns covering a rise they had to cross. The enemy had access to the workings of large iron-ore mines, which shafts and tunnels not only gave them cover but also permitted them to infiltrate back into positions they had lost.

Over on the right flank the Calgary Highlanders attacked May-sur-Orne but after bitter fighting were forced back by powerful counter-attacks. Later the Régiment de Maisonneuve also suffered heavily in an unsuccessful attack on the same objective. The Black Watch of Canada, taking over with an assault on Fontenay-le-Marmion, advanced straight across the high, wide open western end of Verrières Ridge. They came under fire from artillery, mortars and machine-guns from three sides, yet pushed on. Some 60 men reached the crest to run point-blank into a formidable enemy position which included hidden tanks (some disguised as haystacks). Only 15 men survived, and altogether that day the Canadian Black Watch lost 324 men. A squadron of the 1 Hussars who had pushed into May-sur-Orne also suffered heavily. That night the Canadians sustained more severe casualties as they unsuccessfully attempted to storm St Martin, St André-sur-Orne, May-sur-Orne and Fontenay le Marmion.

The failure of the Canadian infantry to tear a hole in the enemy's defences meant there was no opening for the armour. The day's bloody fighting cost the Canadians 1,500 casualties. The 1 and 9 SS Panzer Divisions sent in heavy attacks which were successfully challenged by the Canadian 2 Armoured Brigade and the 7 Armoured Division who, although they lost 56 tanks, inflicted daunting losses on the panzers. Further execution was done by Typhoons and the gains on Verrières ridge were saved. Crouching in their hasty foxholes beneath mind-shattering bombardment it boosted the infantry's morale to see the Typhoons peel off in almost leisurely manner to blast enemy tanks or gun positions.

Montgomery now issued a directive: 'The enemy must be led to believe that we contemplate a major advance towards Falaise and Argentan and he must be induced to build up his main strength to the east of the River Orne, so that our affairs on the western flank can proceed with greater speed.' But the press had become openly sceptical. Stalemate in Normandy was critically mentioned, with dark references to the long, frustrating and costly trench warfare of World War I. Quite unfairly, the slow progress in Normandy was compared with the huge gains by the Red Army on the Russian Front, from which the German High Command had been compelled to switch its main armoured counter-attack force to challenge the menace of Montgomery's British-Canadian army. The American press were the most critical, 'Allies in France Bogged Down on Entire Front' or 'Critic Asserts Americans and British are making a Vice of Overcaution' being typical headlines.

There were also disturbing signs that Eisenhower did not fully understand. As the 'Goodwood' offensive halted he wrote to Montgomery: 'You should insist that Dempsey keeps up the strength of his attack' and that 'in First Army the whole front comes quickly into action to pin down local reserves and to support the main attack'. As Dempsey's British and Canadians had so successfully compelled almost the entire enemy armoured strength to be pitted against them, and most newly committed German infantry, it would seem the Supreme Commander had not really appreciated Montgomery's achievement. The US First Army was supposed to make the *main* attack, and not be 'pinning down local reserves'. That had been more than taken care of, at no little cost to themselves, by the British and Canadians. Yet, according to Lieut General Walter Bedell Smith, his American chief-of-staff, Eisenhower was wanting 'an all-out co-ordinated attack by the entire Allied line . . . He was up and down the line like a football coach, exhorting everyone to aggressive action. But Montgomery was all too aware that to do this would leave nobody with the necessary strength to make a decisive break-through or to exploit it.'

Fortunately Churchill appreciated exactly what Montgomery was doing, and managed to reassure Eisenhower. In addition to all the forces confronting Dempsey's troops at the beginning of July there were now five new infantry divisions and one new armoured division while slightly more than one infantry division and one weak armoured division had reinforced the American front. Eisenhower's misunderstanding was not however as great as that of his British deputy, the RAF Air Chief Marshal Sir Arthur Tedder. He advised Eisenhower to 'put an end to the arrangement by which General Montgomery has operational control of both British and American forces'. Bradley, whose troops had been shouldering into position for Patton's impending break-out, nevertheless fully appreciated. He later wrote: 'Monty's primary task was to attract German troops to the British front that we might more easily secure Cherbourg and get into position for the break-out. In this diversionary mission Monty was more than successful.' Had the American break-out from St Lô begun as intended, on the day after 'Goodwood' started, there could have been no criticism.

On 1 August two brand-new armoured divisions, the 4 Canadian and the 1 Polish, arrived in Normandy. They were to execute the final great break-out from the British sector to trap and destroy the German armies in Normandy or send them reeling back to the Seine. These new arrivals were full of the same confidence that had been inculcated into the D-Day shock troops. They had little conception of the devastation wrought by the German 88mm guns and multi-barrelled mortars, nor of the desperate bravery with which the crack enemy troops were prepared to fight to the death. Certainly these newcomers were over-confident as they took over the heat of the battle from the battered divisions who had been subjected to such prolonged hell. The Poles brought with them the particular bitterness of men who knew that however hard they fought for victory over the hated Germans it could not achieve freedom for their beloved homeland, which must eventually be doomed to subjugation by equally hated Russians.

First the Canadian First Army was to capture Falaise. The massing of the German armour against the British southwards from Mont Pinçon meant the Canadians now faced fewer tanks. Operation 'Totalize' was to be made in three phases, the first to capture Fontenay le Marmion and La Hogue, the second Hautmesnil and St Sylvain and the third was for the Canadian armour to exploit as ordered. The first was to be carried out by the Canadian 2 Armoured Brigade and 2 Infantry Division on the right with the British 33 Armoured Brigade and 51 Highland Division on the left. In the second phase the Canadian 4 Division was to pass through the 2 Division while the 4 Armoured Brigade captured high ground at points 180, 195 and 206 some three miles further on. The Polish Armoured Division on the left was to make a similar advance.

The foremost armoured divisions would for some days be ahead of the main force but it was considered they could well take care of themselves. The dual objective was that the vital Caen–Falaise road would be cut and the main strength of the German armour shattered in repeated counter-attacks. The attack was to open with two columns of armour, and infantry in armoured carriers, advancing through the German front by night, down both sides of the Falaise road. An obliterating raid by 1,000 RAF bombers would account for the enemy defences. Artificial moonlight would be provided by searchlights reflected down from the clouds, Bofors guns would fire tracer to indicate the flanks and the objectives would be marked by green shell bursts. The first wave would be followed early next day by the onrush of the Canadian 4 and Polish 1 Armoured Divisions. The night-charge by the armour was intended to penetrate right to the enemy's rear, so alarming the Germans that they would not be able to concentrate their defences against the following Canadians and Poles. Meanwhile Montgomery had informed his army commanders that all fighting must be to further the American operations. To emphasise that this was the ultimate knock-out punch the French *Maquis* were ordered everywhere to rise against the Germans.

The night attack went very well, thrusting through and home with virtually no enemy fire against the tanks and infantry riding secure in tracked armoured troop-carriers. They charged in six long nose-to-tail four-tank-wide armoured columns, each made up of tanks and flail tanks, infantry in armoured carriers and self-propelled anti-tank guns. They comprised the Canadian 4 Infantry and 2 Armoured Brigades on the west of the Caen–Falaise road, their objective the high ground north of Bretteville-sur-Laize, and on the other side two British brigades, the 154 Highland and 33 Armoured, their objectives the Cramesnil–St Aignan area. Following Canadian and Highland infantry were to capture by-passed enemy strongpoints.

Bert Lawrence, of Ottawa, Canada, then a lieutenant in the 8 Reconnaissance Regiment, took part in the remarkable night charge. Like other Canadian armoured formations, they had until now been used as trench infantry around Caen, Carpiquet and Ifs.

'We were in Bren carriers in a column led by several tanks,' he remembers. 'The massive bombardment in front of us was exciting and reassuring. Then off we clanked into one of the craziest nights I can recall. The countryside was dry as a bone and the bombing and rolling barrage, flail tanks and the combat itself created an enormous dust. As darkness fell the battlefield became almost opaque. There was quite a bit of basically undirected small arms and mortar fire in the air, and although they caused some casualties it did not stop our forward movement. My own column simply kept grinding along.

I [was] more bemused than frightened by the increasing chaos as I ate boiled sweets and chocolate and ducked down for an occasional cigarette. Finally we had no tanks leading us; we could contact no senior officers, our wireless was no help; our maps meant nothing; and morning was approaching. We knew we had passed through a substantial number of Germans during the night but had no idea as to . . . how many we might find around us in the morning. As a result another subaltern and I decided to pull our column into a circle in the tradition of covered waggons under attack by Indians. We had everyone dig holes and drive their carriers over the top. Dawn brought a few German mortar shells but no attack. Very soon hundreds of Germans came straggling towards us and passed us waving pathetic safe conduct leaflets.'

By dawn the columns were firmly established three miles behind the German line. The Canadians, who had encountered more opposition, had not attained all their objectives, but infantry of 51 Highland Division, dismounting at daybreak, swiftly took Garcelles-Secqueville, Cramesnil and St Aignan, with scores of prisoners. The Canadians were established on Point 122, an important hill on the main road near Cramesnil, along the ridge running westwards, and had penetrated to Caillouet. But the ensuing daylight attack was far less lucky. Scheduled also to advance in the wake of mass bombing, they were hit by bombs dropped short by the US Eighth Air Force. Casualties were suffered by a number of units, among them the 51 Highland Division who lost 60 men killed and 300 wounded. An ammunition dump went up and a number of guns were bombed. Determined enemy counter-attacks ensued, particularly on the Scots at St Aignan and on the Canadians on Point 122, but all were repulsed.

Misfortunes were soon being suffered by the Canadian 4 and Polish 1 Armoured Divisions, set to breach the enemy's second defence line between St Sylvian and Bretteville. The 12 SS had not been panicked by the armoured force now behind them and were bitterly contesting the follow-up daylight attack. Because of their inexperience, the attacking divisions did not push on as aggressively as expected. As the Poles debouched from St Aignan, they met head-on a strong German counter-attack, but fought forward to Robertmesnil where they were powerfully challenged by Tigers as they emerged from a wood. Although they knocked out six they were forced to halt.

The Poles had gone into the attack with a controlled fury. They were aware that in Warsaw the Polish resistance had risen. It was only right that the desperation of that struggle should be matched by the fury of the Polish Armoured Division in Normandy. The experience now of the Polish 2 Armoured Regiment was to be the bitter experience of others. As they charged across a wheatfield towards a dark wood, tank after tank was hit by hidden German guns and Panthers. The entire first wave was burning out among the wheat as the second wave went in, flat out. One after another they exploded into smoking pyres. Out of 36 tanks only 10 returned. After them two squadrons of the Polish 24 Lancers advanced across the fated wheatfields in the wake of an attack by the 51 Highland Division. Repeatedly groups of Germans arose in the path of the tanks, some to surrender and others to be gunned down as they hurled grenades and fled. Then the Polish armour was among the Scottish infantry who cheered them, hopeful that the tanks would silence the guns that were so terribly bombarding the fields. But again the Poles were halted. Their onrush split up into a series of attacks by groups of tanks upon German strongpoints in woods, thickets and ruined villages.

The complementary Canadian armoured attack had meanwhile succeeded in capturing Fontenay le Marmion and May-sur-Orne and penetrated as far as Bretteville-sur-Laize. Yet set to cover 16 miles to take Falaise, they had covered no more than 8 and suffered heavy casualties against a formidably armed and dug-down enemy. The 12 SS Panzer Division, possibly the most fanatical of all the young Nazis, had worked feverishly to prepare successive defence lines. There were about 60 dug-down tanks, including Tigers, and self-propelled guns, plus ninety 88mm guns well sited and camouflaged. Manning the defences with 12 SS were 89 Infantry Division, recently arrived from the Pas de Calais, the 272 Infantry Division, and in reserve, the 85 Infantry Division, also from the Fifteenth Army. Westwards, where the British offensive southwards from Caumont was progressing, the Germans were reinforcing what they now believed to be the decisive sector. Von Kluge had ordered Eberbach to move there the II SS Panzer Corps with 9 SS and 10 SS Panzers, the 8 Werfer Brigade, Corps troops and the 660 Heavy Tank Battalion. The 21 Panzer Division was added to II Panzer Corps command. Two more armoured divisions had been diverted from the Americans. Von Kluge reported to High Command: 'The idea of the thrust to Avranches is now scarcely feasible. In the north the English have achieved a very deep penetration astride the Caen–Falaise road.'

12   A Daring Thrust

There were by now over two million Allied and German soldiers locked in the great struggle for Normandy. But in the last 44 days of almost continuous bitter battle in their sector, the British had advanced their front line barely half-a-dozen miles and at a terrible cost. The immediate object of the American break-out was to be the capture of the Brittany ports. Then American reinforcements could be poured in direct across the Atlantic and the whole Allied line would wheel eastwards on the solid pivot of the British position at Caen. That achieved, the Allied armies would advance to engage the Germans in a vast tank battle with their backs to the almost bridgeless Seine.

Montgomery was beginning to shift his weight from Caen to Caumont to drive for the high ground between Vire and the Orne. To continue holding the mass of enemy armour he had set the British Second Army to attack on a front between Caen and St Lô and the Canadians to attack south of Caen towards Falaise. 'Goodwood' had gained sufficient ground for deployment of new divisions. Fully aware of the formidable enemy strength his attacks had drawn in south of Caen, he issued a directive in which he said that 'He is so strong there now that any large-scale operations by us in that area are definitely unlikely to succeed; if we attempt them we would merely play into the enemy's hands, and we would not be helping our operations on the western flank.'

Bradley, now commanding Twelfth Army Group (comprising the US First Army under Lieut General C. H. Hodges and the US Third Army under Patton) was hoping swiftly to encircle the Germans from the south, coming in behind the mass of their armour and fire-power as it faced the British and Canadians. Bitter fighting had resumed on the British front among rolling hills and high-banked little fields, a countryside of orchards, villages and deep ditches suited to defence. As the enemy threw in their full strength to hold the British, the American attack on the right rapidly gained impetus. With the Germans still holding so firmly beyond Caen Montgomery had decided to switch his main blow to Caumont, 50 miles from Caen, at the junction between the British and American armies. There he would pivot the combined wheel. Although aware that this invited a German counter-attack in between the out-thrusting British and American armies, Montgomery did not believe they would attempt it while the bulk of their armour was almost inextricably committed to the Caen battlefield. But Hitler, against the advice of his generals, ordered such a suicidal action.

Between Maltot and Feuguerolles-sur-Orne, the dreaded Tigers fought their last battle for Hill 112. On a perfect summer's day they were caught by the RAF and fled for the cover of woods beneath a searing shower of rockets. Some went up in flames, struck in their less heavily armoured flanks by close-range anti-tank guns hidden among trees. Others were caught in a British artillery bombardment which seemed to be erupting the whole valley of the Orne. It was almost a relief to the Tigers' crews when, on 1 August, the II SS Panzer Corps was ordered to halt a threatened Anglo-American breakthrough at Vire. Dempsey had decided to attack from Caumont with the British VIII Corps on 2 August but the American advance was developing with such speed that Montgomery ordered him to attack on 30 July. He was to both cover part of the American flank and thrust in behind the new front the desperate German Seventh Army was attempting to establish to hold the Americans. On 30 July the British and Americans advanced inexorably from Caumont.

At this dangerous time Trooper Thomson was to have an experience both amusing and rewarding:

'We had spotted a concentration of enemy in and around a village. A small convoy came in sight at the bottom of the valley, all 'soft' vehicles, a staff car, wireless truck and four transports. We withdrew into the trees until they came op-

posite us about 300 yards below, and then opened fire with
machine-guns, knocking out all the vehicles. We saw two
men leave the staff car, each with a small suitcase, and begin
to run across a meadow. Our commander immediately sent
the scout car after them and it brought them back. We found
that the four transports contained rations obviously destined
for German troops we had seen. Of the two men our scout car
had brought back, one was the quartermaster in charge. The
biggest and most pleasurable surprise was that the two suitcases were filled with new French banknotes; obviously it
must have been payday for their troops. We had a big
shareout; everyone received enough to ensure they did not
need to draw any army pay before they were "demobbed"!'

The main British attack was to be by the tanks of VIII
Corps through a gap torn in the enemy defences by the 15
Scottish Division. The armoured cars of the Household Cavalry
led the attack, seeking a weak spot. In such a cramped battlefield the British move, by night, of massive armoured columns,
guns, infantry and supporting vehicles, was fraught with difficulties. New tactics were to be employed now, with tanks and
infantry (often riding on tanks) to fight in close liaison from
field to hedge-hidden field. The Germans were equipped with
yet another new weapon, immense 128mm mobile guns which
wrought a fearful execution among the slow Churchills of the
Scots Guards, accompanying the Scottish infantry. The 11
Armoured Division advanced with 29 Armoured Brigade
Group on the left comprising two armoured regiments, the 3
Royal Tank Regiment and 23 Hussars, with their Rifle Brigade
motor battalion and the 3 Monmouths. On their right was the
armour of the 2 Fife and Forfar Yeomanry and the 2
Northamptonshire Yeomanry plus the infantry of the 4 King's
Shropshire Light Infantry and the 1 Herefords.

Before long the 15 Scottish and 11 Armoured had forced a
gap six miles deep into the German front. They were, however,
dangerously exposed on their left flank where the 43 Wessex
Division were advancing more warily, head-on against the
dominating heights of the Normandy battlefield, topped by

Mont Pinçon. This the Germans must hold if their troops on
the American front were not to be encircled by the British and
Canadians. The looming massif, fronted by an extensive minefield, was manned by crack German infantry in formidable
fortifications with a terrifying backing of artillery. Because
Eberbach was convinced the British were attempting the big
break-through he had moved the 9 SS Panzer Division into
thick woods west of Bretteville-sur-Laize, the 2 Panzers near
them, the 116 Panzer Division east of St Sylvain and had
ordered the 10 SS Panzer Division to Bretteville. On the right,
where 11 Armoured were flanked by the US 5 Infantry Division,
there was strong enemy resistance at Cussy, south-west of
Caumont. The Herefords became involved in a bitter battle in
surrounding woods and the clearing of Cussy caused heavy
casualties before the KSLI and Fife and Forfars could push on
to capture La Baisselière.

Daringly led by a battalion of the Guards Tank Brigade, the
15 Scottish captured high ground dominating St Martin des
Besaces and the KSLI were ordered to push on to take this
village and cut the main road to the west. Through the dangerous darkness they set off in single file along a barely discernible
track and without a shot being fired took the road at dawn. On
the left, meanwhile, in the face of fierce resistance, men of the
Rifle Brigade fought forward to establish themselves along the
railway north and east of St Martin. Then they and the KSLI
made converging attacks to capture the village. The countryside was *bocage* at its most confined with leafy lanes, woodlands,
winding streams and little rivers. Any encounters between
tanks must be head-on, with the massive Tigers and Panthers
dug down and invisible and the advancing Shermans and
Churchills suicidally exposed. The Germans nicknamed the
Shermans 'Tommy Cookers' or 'Ronson Lighters' ('They light
first time'). The slower but more rugged Churchill was not so
quick to burn.

Into this dangerous terrain went the armoured cars of the 2
Household Cavalry. Some soon sinisterly went off the air. But
from one came a message: 'The bridge at 637436 is clear of
enemy and still intact.' This bridge carried the main Le Beny

Bocage–Vire road over the River Souleuvre six miles behind the enemy lines! Lieut D. B. Powle, in an armoured car accompanied by one scout car, had raced down a track through the Forêt L'Evêque after barely evading an 88mm gun. They fell in with an enemy convoy and sped along for two miles close behind in the dust of a German four-wheeled armoured car. When this turned up a side road which crossed the bridge, Powle silently disposed of the German sentry and crossed over to hide the two vehicles in the forest. The six British soldiers thus six miles behind enemy lines then began to send back messages.

The immediate result was dramatic. The entire plan for the advance of VIII Corps was altered and 29 Armoured Brigade was diverted to follow the trail of the two cars. Soon after sunset on 31 July tanks were rumbling over the bridge. The southward thrust across it was to be a turning point in this latest British offensive. By the next day, not only 11 Armoured but the 19 American Division were using the main road which led south-east from the bridge. Inevitably the Germans reacted and soon a strong battle group of 21 Panzer Division was heading for Le Beny Bocage. To deny them the vital bridge an armoured regiment of 11 Armoured Division, infantry clinging to the bucking tanks, raced to the scene. Even as the panzers marshalled in nearby woods they were challenged. In the ensuing bitter battle they were put to flight and next day British armour captured Le Beny Bocage and pushed on towards the Vire. They had driven a significant wedge between the German Seventh Army and Panzer Group West (recently renamed the Fifth Panzer Army). While Hauser was striving desperately to strengthen his left wing against the Americans, the British were threatening to collapse his right.

The British VIII Corps renewed its advance with 11 Armoured pushing out towards Tinchebray and Guards Armoured towards Estry and Vassy. Enemy infantry strongholds and tanks were successively overcome but the opposition intensified. Troops of 11 Armoured took Erouvy on the right and reached the Périers ridge to look down on the Vire–Vassy road between Vire and Chenedolle. The Guards Armoured meanwhile at-

Plate 21. How the Germans hid their heavy tanks – particularly Tigers and Panthers – when using them as fortresses. This one, now knocked out, had been dug down and disguised with sections of a wooden building

Plate 22. British infantry about to ride into battle aboard Sherman tanks, which they increasingly did as the tempo of all-out attack increased

Plate 23. The moment every tank crew feared – as their tank was about to breast a rise and expose its highly armoured underside to enemy high velocity guns. The Sherman tank, seen here, with which the majority of Allied armoured formations were equipped, was in grim jest referred to by Germans as 'the Tommy Cooker'

Plate 24. A British despatch rider stops to inquire the way of American troops as the British assault towards Vire links up with the attacking forces of their allies

Plate 25. When infantry and tanks went in together to take an objective, as at Mont Pinçon, the tank gunners would shell and machine gun enemy positions. The infantry, who would then assault the positions, would meanwhile protect the tanks from being stalked by enemy bazooka parties

tained the high ground above Estry leaving by-passed positions of 21 Panzers to be attacked by following infantry. Challenging this deep penetration 9 SS Panzer Division fought furiously to regain the Périers ridge and the bridge over the Souleuvre. British tanks were within five miles of Vire, the very hub of the Seventh Army's defence against the Americans.

The German command still looked upon the Americans as inferior and considered the British the main danger, and so it was against the Americans that Hitler's great counter-attack was directed. The Germans first had to secure the heights of Mont Pinçon against British attack because to hold the network of roads westwards across this dominating massif was vital. By 2 August reconnaissance revealed the next ridge to the south of the British strongly held by enemy armour. Next day, tanks of the 9 SS Panzer Division drove back advanced British formations from Plesles, but were blasted back by 11 Armoured when they tried to seize the Périers ridge. German infantry began to surge into the terrain immediately ahead of the British salient. Despite attempts by II SS Panzer Corps to break in behind the Périers and Estry ridges the British advanced troops stood firm. The enemy were hurriedly reinforcing east of Vire, the agreed boundary between the British and Americans. Meanwhile west of the town the Americans were breaking through.

Infantry of the British 3 and 43 Divisions were moving forward on each side of the armoured salient ready for an advance. On their left troops of XXX Corps had made less progress. The 43 Division attacking from Bois du Homme beat off a series of attacks by enemy battle groups to advance three miles. They drove soldiers of 21 Panzer Division out of Jurques and captured Hill 301 further south. Then they ran into the newly arrived 10 SS Panzer Division and were halted. To their left 7 Armoured Division had been pushed back almost to Breuil by 10 SS Panzers. The British 50 Division met with better success, fighting forward to seize high ground two miles west of Villers-Bocage. The II Canadian Corps, strengthened by 7 Armoured and Guards Armoured were attacking southwards each side of the Caen–Falaise highroad.

H

It was obvious that the Germans had massed formidable forces against the Canadians and 7 Armoured and Dempsey did not call on them to attack again. They had already fulfilled their role of keeping German armour massed to block the Falaise road, well away from where Operation 'Cobra' was under way with very little to stem its exciting onrush. It had finally opened on 25 July beneath sunny skies. Bradley had listened to Montgomery's advice and concentrated a powerful striking force on a 6,000yd front five miles west of St Lô. Because of the difficulties the American armour had experienced fighting in the *bocage*, von Kluge was expecting their tanks to advance down the available roads and had his anti-tank weapons sited accordingly. He did not know the Americans now had a device (called the 'Rhinoceros') that permitted the tanks to bite through the formidable hedge-topped earth banks. A saw-like row of eight big sharp steel teeth welded to a Sherman tank's front two feet above the ground, it enabled them to drive through a bank at 15mph. Now the American armour could roll forward on a broad front.

13 Happy Valley and Angry Mountain

To a massive opening artillery bombardment nearly 3,000 USAAF bombers added high explosive, fragmentation and napalm bombs on a rectangle of the enemy's defences west of St Lô, five miles long by one mile wide. Although some unfortunately fell short (111 American soldiers were killed and 490 wounded) the great mass struck the Germans. The result, according to the German General Bayerlein, was to devastate an area into 'all craters and death'. He estimated that seventy per cent of the troops were put out of action, either dead, wounded, crazed or stupefied. This was the gap through which Patton's army was to debouch. He had told a press conference that it would fan out in two great spearheads, one to cut off the Brittany peninsula, the other racing east to encircle the German Seventh Army. He declared he would win the war by 11 November because that was his birthday.

To open up the way three tough American infantry divisions had, in twelve days, suffered 10,000 casualties. Their bloody sacrifice secured the four miles' stretch of firm ground along the St Lô Périers road, west of the River Vire, required for launching a massive armoured attack. The sun now shone brilliantly and fighter bombers could give spectacularly effective close support to the clattering tanks and warily advancing infantry. There were visual control posts in leading tanks in verbal communication with aircraft constantly overhead. Streams of bombers and fighters lined up above the battlefield ready to be called down to intervene. On 27 July the Germans cracked and gave way. General Hauser had reported eight days earlier that the infantry holding the main defensive line had become so thin that in further attacks penetrations must inevitably occur. When he told von Kluge that his only reserves were three battalions of infantry and that he must have 'a mobile formation of full fighting strength', von Kluge replied that he could have no armour because the panzer divisions were 'occupied in the main battle area of Caen'. On 30 July the Americans burst through the Avranches bottleneck. Their main strength locked in battle with the British and Canadians, the Germans were in no position to withstand the American attack.

A series of combat command columns plunged forward simultaneously, each with a menacing 'cab rank' of Thunderbolts. They achieved miracles of close support, diving down to destroy enemy strongpoints, tanks and guns, within 100yds of advancing American columns. By the evening powerful columns were swarming down all the main roads between the Vire and Coutances and had advanced 15 miles south. Panzer Group West could send no armour to challenge them. Patton stepped up the already exhilarating pace by despatching his 4 Armoured Division on a 25-mile dash in 36 hours through a gap between the Germans' left flank and the coast. By dark on 30 July they were in Avranches, and had established a bridgehead into Brittany over the River Selune at Pontaubalt. The magnitude of the American break-through, and its exciting immediate potential, was far greater than Omar Bradley had ever envisaged. Indeed, he had planned that when his VII Corps had 'exploited' as far as Coutances and Brehal there would be a phase of consolidation followed by combined pressure over a broad front.

The powerful punch, quickly developing into a penetrating thrust, such as Patton was now delivering, was more in the style of Montgomery than of Eisenhower or Bradley. Indeed Montgomery had stipulated that once the Americans had begun their offensive there must be no pause until it had driven south beyond Avranches and Mortain and had swung up on to the line Caumont–Fougères, to be fast followed by 'a wide sweep south . . . to Le Mans–Alençon'. Von Kluge immediately realised the significance of Patton's spectacular advance. 'The whole western front has been ripped open,' he warned the German High Command. 'The left flank has collapsed.' And because the infinitely more powerful right flank was even now in imminent danger of disintegration beneath the hammer blows of the British and Canadians, there was no hope at all of the Germans providing reserves to try to stem the American armoured tide. The British and Canadians were compelling von Kluge to keep his formidable armour and artillery committed against them.

Patton, never disposed to bother over much about his flanks, was well aware that such enemy troops as there were in Brittany were mostly concentrated in the ports. Enemy strongpoints he might by-pass he knew would be contained by the very active French Resistance. Indeed, the only appreciable German reaction to Patton's swift advance was to direct the entire available bomber force, such as it was, to attack the bridge at Avranches, the most vulnerable point in the US Third Army's line of advance. In the face of constant attack by Allied fighters and formidable anti-aircraft fire, the German bombers scored only one glancing blow and never even caused the flow of armour and motorised infantry to pause. Patton urged no less than seven divisions, vehicles nose to tail, through this bottleneck inside 72 hours. Ahead of the American armour, two armoured and one motorised infantry divisions, lay open terrain, wonderful tank country for a commander of daring not prepared to count the costs overmuch. The records show Patton 'disappeared in a cloud of dust'. 'Suddenly the war became fun,' wrote American war correspondent James Wellard, attached to the US Third Army. 'It became exciting, carnivalesque, tremendous. It became victorious and even safe.'

It was in the beginning almost ridiculously easy; it was delirious, thrilling, magnificent, riding high as conquering heroes, with hardly any danger to mar their onrush. With the American 4 Armoured Division leading they roared along the Lessay–Coutances road, hurtling pell-mell through the Lessay Gap down along the splendid coastal highway through Coutances and Avranches to burst out from that gateway with the whole interior of France before them. Wide, green, verdant countryside; broad, metalled roads; a splendid area of France practically devoid of any natural obstacles or enemy troops, stretched before them as though there was nothing to stop them until the German frontier. That was how they felt as they plunged forward, and that was how it was largely to prove. 'I had the impression . . . of reliving the 1940 situation but in reverse—total chaos among the enemy, complete surprise of his columns,' General Phillipe Leclerc, heroic leader of the Free French 2 Armoured Division, informed General de Gaulle.

'General Leclerc set a pattern of action for his division,' remembers Tony Triumpho, from Canajoharie, New York, a lieutenant in an American artillery battery with the Free French. 'He would have a meeting of his officers to set out his own battle plan. Invariably he would say: "Our objective is there but we will go on to here because I will contact my friend the mayor, or a friend in the underground, who will order a feast to be prepared for us." Leclerc always adapted the corps plan to suit his own type of fighting of "liberating and celebrating". After taking an objective, there would be a splendid meal with wine and champagne.'

Vivid memories of those heady days of 'liberating and celebrating' were also retained by Thomas E. Cassidy from Illinois. Then a captain in the US 3 Armoured Division, he remembers that Leclerc's division 'were intoxicated with . . . fighting . . . on French soil in the midst of a great American army. I saw French soldiers spread over the fields, and spilling in and out of houses, and bivouacked *with camp fires going*, and singing, and feasting, and wine flowing. The whole scene . . . might have occurred in another age—we were not even shelled that night!'

General Patton was hurling his whole magnificent army at the enemy, through a bottleneck which according to the book was far too narrow and dangerous. He later wrote: 'The plans when they came into my mind seemed simple but after I had issued orders and everything was moving, and I knew that I had no reserve, I had a feeling of worry and had to say to my-self "do not take counsel of your fears". If I had worried about flanks I could never have fought the war.' In three days

Patton's armoured columns were able to race on 75 miles, deep into the rear of von Kluge's armies, almost reaching Le Mans. The sort of thing that was happening in the Germans' rear meanwhile was described by American war correspondent Wellard thus:

'A column of seventy German vehicles had been ambushed by a single American medium tank and the whole seventy tanks, field guns, half tracks, ambulances, trucks, private cars, the General's caravan—in fact, the entire headquarters column of an SS panzer division—had been methodically knocked out. A regiment of armoured infantrymen of the American division [4 Armoured] had completed the destruction of the SS column after the Sherman had knocked out the lead tank. The Germans had been trapped in the narrow road, unable to turn, unable to escape into the flanking fields because of the high, thick hedges. They had fought to the death. It became evident as we went further in the wake of the 4 Armoured Division, that a major disaster was beginning to overtake the Reichswehr.'

But no such signs of disaster were apparent along the front where the British and Canadians were locked in battle with the enemy's armoured might. Although von Kluge had ordered Panzer Group West to withdraw to a line from Thury-Harcourt (on the Orne) to Vire, the British XII Corps' pursuit was anything but swift. Mines and booby traps were thick along the enemy's route and by the evening of 4 August the British centre had only reached Evrecy, their left flank was near Armaye on the Orne, and the right had joined troops of XXX Corps entering the ruins of Villers-Bocage. Next day, confronted by fewer mines and only moderate infantry resistance some columns covered up to seven miles and by nightfall the British line ran from the loop of the Orne near Thury-Harcourt, westwards round to where it faced the formidably steep Mont Pinçon.

These abrupt heights were not the only obstacle. The valley of the Orne on the 59 Division's front was deep with steep slopes along much of the western side so that the only approaches for tanks and other vehicles were down roads leading to bridges which had been blown. On the far side the terrain was eminently suitable for defence, with many farms, orchards and small villages extending back to undulating hills and the Forêt de Grimbosq. Infantry began to wade the river near Brieux at dusk on 6 August. Three battalions were across by daylight and soon cleared the enemy sufficiently for engineers to bridge the Orne, despite heavy mortaring. A squadron of tanks had meanwhile found a ford, to the relief of the infantry over the other side who had sighted Tigers and were being counter-attacked.

A strong battle group of the 12 SS Panzer Division roared across from the Canadian sector. Furious fighting ensued for 24 hours, but the issue was finally decided by a crescendo of artillery fire upon the enemy concentrations. The Orne bridgehead was firmly held. Further west 7 Armoured Division advanced to the high ground east of Aunay-sur-Odon and prepared to push on southwards, but Mont Pinçon barred the way. For the assault on this formidable height a brigade group comprising 129 Brigade and the 13/18 Hussars was sent forward. As they approached the villages of St Jean le Blanc and La Varinière, and a stream which skirted the two villages, they became involved in desperate fighting. St Jean le Blanc was a key position in Panzer Group West's new defence line and eight infantry battalions were concentrated there on a four-mile front. The commander of the 15 Division decided to send in the main attack on the west face of Mont Pinçon, reinforced by bringing the 130 Brigade from Ondefontaine to assault the north face. Ondefontaine had been captured by the 43 Division after a day and a night of furious fighting. They were involved in more now as they battled their way towards the northern slopes of Mont Pinçon.

Mont Pinçon is 1,200ft high, and its sides are very steep. The weather was hot and close, threatening thunder. Dust, stirred up by moving vehicles, bursting shells, marching feet, hung chokingly heavy upon the fetid air. Behind a heavy barrage soldiers of the Wiltshire Regiment moved forward. Under the vicious fire of machine-guns and mortars the two leading companies visibly withered away. To the north, half a mile away, the Somersets were similarly mown down. But at La Varinière two tanks of the 13/18 Hussars raced across a bridge, to be followed by six more and 60 surviving Wiltshires. They charged through a strong force of Germans in an orchard, shooting many down, and swiftly secured the vital crossroads at La Varinière. Leaving the near-exhausted infantry, seven Hussars tanks clattered up the hill along a rough track above a sheer drop, took the Germans by surprise, and reached the top. Soon the rest of the squadron joined them.

When the Brigade Commander saw the tanks silhouetted against the sky he ordered another battalion of the Wiltshires to follow them. Although exhausted from the savage battle at St Jean le Blanc these infantrymen set off in single file up precipitous thorny slopes to the amazement of the German soldiers they passed. Above them, as they climbed, they heard the rushing of the shells of their own artillery barrage. Bursts of machine-gun and rifle fire came from both sides all along the length of the hill beyond them. By nightfall the Wiltshires were digging in on their side of the crest around the tanks, and could hear the enemy digging in on the other side. A thick fog had come down on and around the hilltop, shrouding all. The British and German positions were so close that they could hear each other talking. Under cover of darkness, more Shermans of the Hussars pushed forward to climb up among the infantry. While the infantry protected them from being stalked by enemy bazooka parties, the tank soldiers machine-gunned identified enemy positions. When the fog cleared early next day the enemy positions were assaulted and overcome. Soon 130 Brigade fought up the north face. The British presence on Mont Pinçon had laid open the German defences.

On the British right meanwhile the armoured divisions of VIII Corps were fighting bitterly to retain their positions on the Périers ridge. The enemy had powerfully reinforced his Chenedolle stronghold and developed Estry as a formidable position. There the 9 SS Panzers were holding the 15 Scottish Division with dug-in tanks and batteries of 88mm guns and *nebelwerfers*. On the other flank the 3 Division had met with more success, having captured Montisanger and le Houden-guerie and had crossed the Allière to reach the high ground north of the railway to Vire where they made contact with American troops. Montgomery had issued orders for the advance to the Seine, even though not clear what the enemy intended to do. He was certain they intended holding the ground east, south-east and south of Caen, for they were fighting back there with a ferocious desperation. A particularly determined attack was made on the British positions on Périers ridge by the 10 SS Panzer Division, switched from Aunay-sur-Odon. But everywhere the British soldiers fought back with such determination that the panzer troops were beaten back before nightfall. Their casualties were increased by RAF fighter bombers.

Although the Allied aircraft were continuing to dominate the battlefield (9 SS Panzer Division, for instance, had taken a night and a day to move 30 miles) they were continually suffering casualties. The Luftwaffe had been virtually destroyed, but German anti-aircraft defences remained formidable, particularly at river crossings and road junctions. In one attack by Allied medium bombers on a column of tanks between Argentan and Flers, 6 out of 28 were shot down. And in a daylight attack by 54 Mitchell medium bombers on massing panzers at Grimbosq no less than 36 were badly damaged by flak, some having to make forced landings.

Fighting erupted with a new violence in the Orne bridge-head and along the Falaise road. The 59 Staffordshire Division was ordered to develop the bridge-head a few hours after the capture of Mont Pinçon. The infantry made assault crossings and then the Royal Engineers bridged the Orne during the night. The enemy responded with a terrible artillery barrage and soon a battle group of the 12 SS, backed by Tigers, made a strong counter-attack. 'We took a terrible pasting as we approached the river down a long unsheltered slope in full view of a well entrenched enemy,' remembers Ernest Ambler, of Bridgend, Mid Glamorgan. 'Our armour was being knocked out before it reached the river. What little got across received similar treatment as it climbed the opposite slope.' But the tenacious Staffordshire infantry held their ground despite dreadful casualties which, in some rifle companies, amounted to over ninety per cent.

Always there was the earthquaking support of the artillery, some of whose guns were firing 1,000 rounds a day until their barrels turned incandescent blue. Whole fields, formidable with dug-down German armour, machine-gunners and infantry, erupted as massive concentrations of fire from all calibres of artillery, along with shells from warships, burst upon them. So bitter was the bombardment upon unyielding British infantry and unrelenting German attack that it seemed this part of the great battle of Normandy would only be decided when every man was dead on one side. The British bridge-head across the Orne remained utterly precarious.

14 The Mad Charge

Despite the savage enemy attacks in the British sector strong panzer forces moved westwards across the Orne to challenge the by now appreciated threat of Patton's break-out. Hitler's edict was that eight of the nine panzer divisions engaged by the British and Canadians must smash through from Vire–Mortain to the coast at Avranches. Every aircraft the Luftwaffe had available would be thrown in. Although both von Kluge and Hauser knew this was inviting the total destruction of the German Seventh Army, they dared not disobey. Since the attempt on Hitler's life on 20 July German generals had been executed at an alarming rate! Von Kluge ordered the full force of the German armour to drive all-out for Avranches on the night of 6/7 August. But to execute the order was another thing. Patton's foremost tanks were bearing down on Le Mans and the 9 Panzer Division was despatched to stop them. Patton was now making four clearly defined thrusts. One was due west towards Brest, another south-west towards L'Orient, a third south to St Nazaire and the fourth east and south-east to the Seine and Paris. The German General Staff wrongly calculated that Patton's main intention was to seize the Brittany ports, but he had split his formidable army into two and the more powerful part was now moving eastwards.

Patton's columns were everywhere causing confusion behind the enemy lines. The fact that his racing armoured divisions were virtually out of his control, being mostly out of contact with his HQ, did not in any way detract from their deadly effectiveness. His main force heading eastwards and now swinging north towards Falaise was to cover 170 miles in 12 days. 'Go where you can, as fast as you can' were Patton's somewhat unmilitary orders. Leclerc took his French 2 Armoured Division

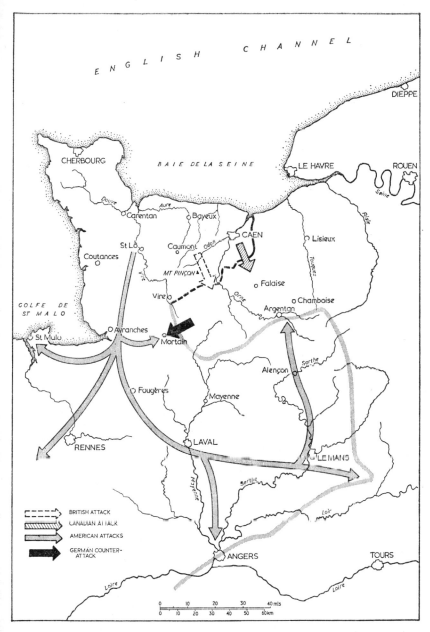

Map 5   Creating the Falaise pocket 13 August

on a furious charge towards Falaise that covered 70 miles in 24 hours!

Meanwhile, so fiercely were the British attacking (this was the day of the Mont Pinçon battle) that to disengage the five panzer divisions ordered westwards was quite impossible. In fact, only the 1 SS Panzer Division could be withdrawn. What was to have been a devastating blow towards Avranches by eight armoured divisions was reduced to a thrust by four divisions with only 250 tanks between them, so terrible had been the attrition in the desperate fighting to hold the British. And Omar Bradley was ready for them, deploying five infantry divisions, with two armoured combat commands in reserve, along an 18-mile front between Vire and Mortain. He virtually lined with steel and guns the narrow corridor along which the enemy must advance. He called in three of Patton's divisions from Brittany to concentrate in a 'back stop' position west of Mortain. With the direct route to Avranches thus barred, Bradley began to strike sharply at the flanks of the German salient.

Bradley sent his VII Corps' mobile forces around the enemy's flank to Amrières and Mayenne to link up with the Third Army and directed his most powerful blow against Vire, the main bastion of the German Seventh Army's right flank. The British Second Army at the same time punched hard towards that town. The Germans counter-attacked with part of the armoured force meant to blast through to Avranches, but could not prevent the Americans not only capturing Vire but also overrunning a part of the chosen start-line, east of St Pois, for the main German onslaught. When that night the 2 Panzers broke through between Mortain and Sourdeval, to push on seven miles towards Avranches, they were soon stopped by the US 3 Armoured Division. The enemy recaptured Mortain but could advance no further in the face of determined opposition by the US 30 Division. The 2 Panzers endeavoured to continue their advance under cover of morning mist but when it lifted RAF Typhoons and USAAF Thunderbolts soon discovered them. With the summer skies now fine and clear from 5 am to 10pm, the Allied fighter-bombers had a full 17 hours in each day to attack the enemy. That afternoon the 47 Panzer Corps pro-

tested to Seventh Army: 'The activities of the fighter bombers
are almost unbearable.'

The 1 SS Panzer Division's attack was halted. That of the
116 Panzer Division never even started. They had been rushed
in, along with the 84, 89 and 363 Infantry Divisions and
elements of 6 Parachute Division from north of the Seine. The
German High Command had finally relaxed their guard at the
Pas de Calais. Instead of the Fifteenth Army being used to
provide a firm base on which the defeated Normandy troops
could re-form, these new formations were, on Hitler's insistence,
launched into the fatal Mortain attack. The 2 Panzers were
stunned by the ferocity of the RAF Typhoons which rocketed
to a burning shambles one enemy column of 60 panzers and
200 vehicles. The thousand Luftwaffe fighters ordered in were
assailed by Allied fighters from take-off. General Hans von
Funck, commander of the 47 Panzer Corps, reported: 'The
situation of our tanks is becoming very alarming. The 116 has
not advanced one step today, neither have the other units.'
Bradley now sent in a perfectly timed counter-attack, and on 7
August a combat command of the US 2 Armoured struck
swiftly through St Hilaire to Barentin, thence into the enemy's
rear at Mortain. Patton's Third Army meanwhile was pushing
on purposefully southwards to Angers and eastwards to Le
Mans. Suddenly the long-term threat of envelopment had become a very imminent danger for the German Seventh Army.

That morning a shot-down American pilot rescued by the
French Resistance reported to Patton's HQ that he had driven
from Angers to Châteaubriant without seeing any Germans but
a few signallers retreating. Patton immediately despatched a
combat team to attack Angers. He then displayed a measure
of caution by stopping the 80 and 35 Infantry Divisions and
the French 2 Armoured near St Hilaire after hearing that
German panzer divisions were about to attack westwards. Apparently with little conception of what it was like to fight against
the full strength of the German armour, Patton noted that at
this time he stopped sending back position reports 'in case some
directive-reading S.O.B. should tell me "Patton, you've already
reached your designated objective, so stop there and await

further orders".' He added: 'Why, hell! the only thing for an
army to do when it has the enemy on the run is to keep going
until it runs out of gas, and then continue on foot to keep killing
until it runs out of ammunition, and then to go on killing with
bayonets and rifle butts . . .'

It was obvious that there was little to stop Patton. On their
whole southern front of 100 miles from Domfront through Le
Mans to the Loire at Angers, the Germans had only the 9
Panzer Division, one infantry division and six security battalions. Yet on 8 August von Kluge, in blind obedience to
Hitler, ordered the 9 Panzers to make a further attempt to
smash through to Avranches. The despairing Hauser pro-
tested: 'This will deal a death blow not only to the Seventh
Army but to the entire Wehrmacht in the West.' The next 48
hours finally settled their fate in Normandy. Jubilant at the
manner in which Hitler was ordering his armies into a deadly
trap, Montgomery changed his plan from a long hook, to be
strengthened by the dropping of an airborne force, to block the
enemy's line of retreat through the gap between the Seine at
Paris and the Loire at Orléans. Instead he ordered a short hook
to bring the Canadians and Americans together around
Argentan to trap the enemy there.

It was the need to close the trap that prompted the Canadians
now to mount a headlong charge upon the terrifying array of
German anti-tank guns drawn across their path. The code
name for this attack was 'Tractable' but the troops were soon
calling it 'The Mad Charge'. It was to open with another
massive bombing attack by Bomber Command's night bombers
along both flanks of the corridor of advance with smoke bombs
among the high explosives to blind the enemy gunners. The
Canadian tanks were to charge in two simultaneous waves, 160
in the first and 90 in the second, closely followed by infantry in
armoured carriers. The sun shone on the waves of ripening
wheat through which the tanks rumbled forward at midday on
14 August. But soon the bombers obliterated it with a towering
pall of smoke and dust. When the sun re-emerged as a glowing
red circle through the sulphurous fog, the tank commanders
took it as a marker and drove towards it.

Plate 26. Tanks of the Canadian armoured divisions set off on 'The Mad Charge', with which it was intended to close the trap on the Germans at Falaise. Note the flail tank in the foreground, used to beat the ground with revolving chains to explode mines

Plate 27. A section of a long file of German prisoners moving into the rear area after coming out to surrender as the 'Mad Charge' of the Canadian armour roared through their positions

Plate 28. The inferno of the Falaise gap as the Allied guns bombarded the fleeing Germans and the Allied fighters and fighter-bombers attacked them without ceasing. This is a view of the holocaust from the Canadian sector

Plate 29. A small section of the road below the Polish hilltop position at Coudehard, where the Polish guns decimated a close packed German column of tanks, guns, and motor and horse transport

The tanks charged, bucking and lurching flat-out across country, their gunners as blinded to the enemy as the German anti-tank gunners were to them. Although every hedge was stiff with enemy guns, and machine-gunners lurked in the corn, the blind charge of the Canadian armour hurtled on, firing on everything that looked like an enemy gun position. The infantry followed, straight through two German infantry divisions newly arrived from Norway. Far ahead RAF rocket-firing fighters sought out the German long-range gun positions. Nevertheless, despite the smoke-screen, German guns took an increasing toll of the onrushing Canadians.

There were two thrust lines: on the right 3 Division and 2 Armoured Brigade and on the left 4 Division and 8 Infantry Brigade. The experiences of 4 Brigade were typical as, behind powerful artillery and air bombardments, they moved forward through a narrow corridor between smoke-screens. On the left were the Canadian Grenadiers and on the right the Foot Guards. Close behind were the Lake Superior and British Columbia Regiments. A squadron of flail tanks was under command. Huge clouds of chalk dust which merged with drifting smoke enveloped them. After some two miles they were among enemy infantry outposts, which they charged and heavily machine-gunned. Then the first line of anti-tank guns opened up and the air was filled with the rushing of high-velocity armour-piercing projectiles, the roar of the guns following. Tank after tank shuddered beneath the impact, burst into flame, billowed acrid smoke. Still tanks rolled on. By Quesnay wood, a large wood which split the Canadian line, a strongpoint of panzers, anti-tank guns and machine-gun nests protected by a minefield, confronted them. More Canadian tanks were shattered and survivors banded together as infantry and continued to attack. Germans began to surrender.

As the Canadian armoured wave breasted a rise to begin a long descent to the River Laison, they saw hundreds of German dead strewn across the fields, smashed anti-tank guns and exploding ammunition dumps. German soldiers began to come towards them in droves in surrender. The river-crossing was perilous beneath the savage fire of anti-tank guns. A crossing

I

place was discovered near Rouvres, where inevitable congestion developed. As German MkIVs came in a series of battles developed. Tanks of the Foot Guards fought forward to the high ground at Olendon which was very strongly held. An absolute fury of gunfire erupted there and many tanks on both sides were aflame, the air choked with smoke, dust and cordite fumes, the ground littered with the dead of both sides. German prisoners were taken in large numbers. When darkness fell, livid with leaping flames, the Canadians pulled out from the confusion to re-form west of Sassy.

Typical of the harrowing experiences of many Canadian tank soldiers was that of Neil Stewart, from Ottawa, with the Canadian Grenadier Guards. He recalls the Sherman tank in which he was loader-operator, commanded by Sgt Sandy Forsyth, with driver Leo Godall, bow gunner Russell Scott and gunner Bill Brown:

'We were all a little strung up because we had to make a frontal assault upon well prepared positions in broad daylight. We had been told that the German defences were several miles thick and that we should have to ram our way at least six miles forward to take on easier targets in their rear. We were buoyed, however, by the sheer number of tanks, half-tracks and weapon carriers surrounding us, and by the promise of a smoke-screen. We were not convinced that the heavy bomber raids had seriously disrupted the German defences, having had experience closer to Caen.

'We charged down a hill in the centre of the mass of tanks. The smoke-screen seemed relatively ineffectual as the wind bore it quickly away. To our intense dismay there was a small stream at the foot of the hill which had apparently escaped notice on the maps. Tanks circled around frantically searching for a crossing place. After some short delay the tanks and other vehicles were able to cross but our formations had been seriously disrupted. We all concluded that, wherever we found ourselves in relation to other formations, we had to "go and go hard" toward the sun, which was toward Falaise. Dust and smoke swirled everywhere as random targets were fired upon ... With my vision limited to an occasional glimpse out of my periscope it was a wild and bumpy ride through what was obviously a very beautiful countryside.

'Our squadron had spread out widely. Close control had been lost at the crossing of the creek, and tanks simply roared toward the sun. I could see several hit and burning, and a number of wrecked German anti-tank guns. But we could not yet see any German tanks. Sandy Forsyth took us, along with a number of other tanks, along the left side of the attack line and into a large wheat field. We shot up some German infantry and a frantic "88" crew trying to get their gun into action in our direction. We could hear heavy artillery shells exploding to our left front, as the Canadian and British guns hammered the German positions.

'About one hour after the charge started, our luck changed. I saw two or three tanks burning very close to us. Crews still alive were scrambling out and flopping down into the wheat to hide from fire from woods to our left. Then a gush of blood from the open hatches of our turret marked the end of Sandy Forsyth. An armour-piercing shot had hit him squarely in the face. His large body, decapitated as if by a great cleaver, slumped to the turret floor amid the spent shell casings, his own blood and fragments of his head. Within a few more seconds the tank shuddered and stopped. Smoke poured in from the engine and a tongue of flame leaped along the drive shaft below us. We had taken a shell in the engine compartment. I can still remember our gunner, Bill Brown, leaning back into the turret to help me get out. I had to crawl under the master gun, over Sandy's remains and out the hatch. The lanyard of my pistol had fouled the gun and Bill gave me a great yank and pulled me free. We both scrambled down into the wheat, where we were joined by Leo and Russell from the forward compartment.'

That night, by the time the 'Mad Charge' had ended, the Canadians were still short of Falaise and the vital high ground dominating the Germans' escape gap. They had, however, captured Sassy and Olendon and adjacent high ground. What had happened to Stewart and his comrades, meanwhile, was again an experience shared by many Canadian tank soldiers that day:

'We lay for a while in the tracks in the wheat made by other tanks. We soon realised that we were attracting machine-gun fire from the woods to our left. We scattered down various tracks in the wheat to get away from the knocked-out tanks. A pause in the firing followed, during which we could hear commands in German being given as an enemy infantry sweep was organised to clean us out of the field. We had nothing but pistols to defend ourselves now, with well armed infantry approaching. One soldier saved the bacon for all of the twenty-odd tank men now crawling around desperately in the wheat. Despite accurate sniper fire he stood up behind a knocked-out tank, took the spare 30-calibre Browning machine-gun stored in the blanket box at the rear and quickly began firing at the approaching German infantry. The Germans instantly realised that this was not going to be an easy shoot-up of helpless grounded tank men after all, and withdrew hastily to the woods.

'Desultory sniping continued throughout the hot afternoon, some by anti-tank guns looking for any target whatever. One shot took the leg of Russell Scott. None of us knew where our lines were. About 5 o'clock a trio of Germans emerged from the woods carrying a white flag and gave us to understand that we could surrender, or we were to be wiped out by an attack from all the Germans to our rear. An artillery officer from a Canadian regiment, who had joined us after losing his vehicle and crew, told them in rather rude terms to "beat it". They soon withdrew and the promised attack did not materialise. We became more optimistic about our chances. We seemed to be attracting less fire from the nearby woods. We crawled toward a line of bushes to our rear but a "moaning minnie" opened up on them. Since we had not crawled that far we avoided a deadly working over. Around us about eight or ten tanks steadily burned while explosions marked the end of their ammunition. Several among us were wounded, some quite painfully. The conviction grew that after dark we should travel towards the sound of the heaviest artillery fire, which should be our own lines. About 7.30, three German tanks lumbered out of the trees about 400 yards away. They stopped, and the crews dismounted. A pair of the twin-bodied Lockheed P-38 1 Lightnings wheeled high overhead while the German tank men vainly fired machine-guns towards them. Then darkness mercifully surrounded us, broken here and there by the fires that still burned from the wrecked tanks.

'We set off, trying to walk in the ruts left by the tanks to reduce the risk from mines. One of our number who strayed off was badly wounded in the leg when an "S" mine exploded. After perhaps an hour of wary creeping in the dark we saw silhouetted against a fire the outline of a small but heavily armed German patrol. They had heard us beyond doubt. I will always recall the cold sweat while we waited silently for their next move. After a few minutes they moved off and we did likewise, breathing again. We took heart as we covered more distance. Suddenly a fighter plane of unknown origin dropped a parachute flare which brilliantly lit up our surroundings. Apparently the pilot could see more than we thought he could for we immediately became the target of a series of wicked machine-gun bursts. Fortunately, nobody was hurt and we slogged forward. Then we began to fear an encounter with our own infantry. We resolved that we would talk and make noises to indicate we were not stealing up. About 1 o'clock we heard in a thick Scottish brogue "Who goes ther-r-e?" We were delighted to inform an outpost of the 51 Highland Division that we were Canadians.'

The Canadians passed a tense night, savaged by shell fire. The Foot Guards had suffered more than most, though all had sustained heavy casualties. Yet next morning, 15 August, the Canadian Army pushed on once more. On the outskirts of Epancy they again came under heavy fire and in subsequent bitter duels still more tanks were lost while inflicting heavy losses. The Canadians' objective was now within range of their guns and the enemy retaliated with an even more furious barrage. German guns in Falaise itself were now bombarding them.

The Canadians had completely overrun the first enemy gun line with both infantry and armour, and the 3 Division was within three miles of Falaise. But the battlefield was hideous with burned-out Canadian tanks and shattered German guns and strewn with charred and distorted dead of both sides. Many of the casualties sustained by the Canadian Guards were caused when they sought to by-pass Quesnay Wood, reportedly lightly held but in fact the very heart of the German anti-tank screen. At the end of this brutal day one squadron had lost 12 of its 19 tanks and two others 14 between them. The British Columbia Regiment, also heading for Point 195, had been wiped out. Next day, the Canadian Guards managed to reach Hill 195 despite again sustaining casualties from 88mms, Tigers and mortars. The Argyll and Sutherland Highlanders dug in around the hill to provide defence. Meanwhile heavy fire from Canadian tanks and artillery and rocketing by RAF Typhoons scarified Quesnay Wood. Although by 15 August the Canadians had still not taken the vital last ridge they were thrusting determinedly into the old town of Falaise. The massive Norman castle, birthplace of William the Conquerer, was itself in the firing line, though the 12ft thick stone walls remained almost impervious to the shells.

The 1 Polish Armoured Division had fought down from Robertmesnil to take St Sylvain, Cauvicourt and Soignolles. But yet another enemy anti-tank screen, stiff with 88mms, halted their progress. Their immediate objective was Hill 140.

'The Hill was clearly visible and the Germans there could see us clearly too,' noted the 1 Polish Armoured Division's historian. 'We were driving a wedge into the German defences. The defenders, well dug in on both sides of the wedge, rained a deadly fire on us. The wheat began to burn, the smoke spreading over the field like an umbrella. The heat was suffocating. Through his field glasses Major Stefanowicz

could clearly see Shermans on the slopes of Hill 140. Every
few moments one burst into flames. The 4th Canadian Division, engaged on the hill, lost 47 (out of 60) tanks. The
Commanding Officer knew that a direct attack over that
cemetery of Canadian tanks would be madness. He decided
to manoeuvre in the direction of the adjacent Hill 111.
Bartosinski's Shermans, like dogs straining at the leash, leapt
forward and threshing the wheat with their tracks, opened a
devastating fire with guns and machine-guns. They moved
up the hill where there were masses of deeply dug holes.
Germans emerged and ran in front holding up their hands.
In the bushes were some smashed-up guns. Sometimes, at
rare intervals, volleys of Spandau fire were heard. The anti-
tank guns were silent. Lieut Kawalczyk reported that the
1st Squadron had struck a minefield and had come in for a
hail of anti-tank shells. The 3rd troop, under Second Lieut
Zaremba, had been literally shot to pieces. Lieut Limburger
had reached Hill 111 with only 7 tanks. Dusk was falling.
We must hurry . . .'

That night it was decided the attempt to breach the German
defences with tanks was too costly. The 3 Infantry Brigade
went into the attack upon St Sylvain. The Germans established
a new line along the River Laison and through the Quesnay
woods. Against this the Poles flung themselves with fury, but
could not break through. The Canadian 4 Armoured Division
on their right were also halted by 88mms as they attempted to
advance further after taking Bretteville le Rabet. They were
embroiled in heavy fighting as the Germans repeatedly counter-
attacked. The Canadian 3 Infantry Division came up under
cover of darkness to relieve the battered armour and a formation of the 4 Armoured then made a daring thrust in between
the German defences at Grainville Langannerie and Quesnay.
When dawn broke a brigade of Canadian armour was established on Point 195 and high ground near Laize. Inevitably a
series of fierce enemy counter-attacks came in, all of them
beaten off. That evening the Canadian infantry twice attacked
a formidable enemy redoubt in the Quesnay woods, but after

bitter close-quarters fighting were compelled to withdraw. The German defences had just been reinforced by the 85 Infantry Division from the Fifteenth Army.

The heavy bombers gave their formidable attention to Quesnay woods: 1,200 roared inexorably across the cloudless sky in a seemingly endless stream. First a Mosquito dropped smoke bombs to indicate the target. Then the huge bombs came tumbling down and the ground trembled as fountains of earth and dust arose from the wood, amidst it splintered and even whole trees and chunks of masonry from shattered defence positions. Then, unaccountably, one bomber diverged to drop its load on the village of Couvicourt, where formations of the Polish 1 Armoured Division were waiting to make a follow-up assault. The column of smoke which arose attracted other bombers and Polish vehicles in the streets and fields and orchards were soon in flames and many men had been killed and wounded. They were saved from further devastation by the pilot of an artillery observation aircraft, who spiralled upwards before the advancing bombers firing Very lights. When the Poles did attack the shattered wood a ferocious fire came from surviving German positions as Polish infantry attacked them with the bayonet. Dreadful casualties were sustained on both sides. The Poles had to withdraw, carrying their many wounded through burning wheatfields. But that night, as the Very lights of the Allied forward troops soared into the sky on three sides of the Germans, it became apparent to them that they were virtually surrounded.

15 The Tumultuous Cauldron

The German Seventh Army, Panzer Group West and Panzer Group Eberbach, were hemmed into a narrow salient, everywhere menaced by British, Canadian, Polish, American and French guns and armour and by the concentrated fury of the multitude of Allied aircraft. The British Second Army were exerting increasing pressure: the 59 Division had established a bridge-head at Thury-Harcourt, Villers-Bocage was securely in British hands and 7 Armoured were in Aunay-sur-Odon, five miles further south. The Army's plan now was to exploit their Orne bridge-head by advancing on both sides of that river, striking out south and south-east. The 11 Armoured Division was to lead, clearing as it progressed. Once the enemy was obviously in full retreat the armour would boldly by-pass enemy troops less than a company strong, leaving them to be mopped up by infantry.

The American First Army meanwhile was remorselessly destroying the enemy salient west of Mortain. On the German southern flank Eberbach's Panzer Group was fighting desperately. It was perfectly clear to Montgomery that the enemy was intending to evacuate the armour and leave the infantry. That the retreat was becoming disorganised was proved by the identification of elements of no less than eleven different divisions near Argentan. British and American forces were everywhere along both sides of the pocket, battering inwards. Although Patton had been urging his troops to storm Falaise from the south, Bradley had ordered them to halt at Argentan. Patton angrily disagreed with Bradley's contention that they might collide disastrously with the British advance and asserted that his formations 'could easily have entered Falaise and closed the gap'. But although Haislip's three available divisions

153

were obviously strong enough to form a powerful shoulder on the southern side of the Falaise gap, they were certainly not strong enough to plug it. Meanwhile to have reinforced Haislip must have been to the considerable detriment of the US Third Army's dramatic race for Paris and the Seine, even then developing excitingly.

The German armies were indeed in a precarious position. Hitler, still insisting on continuation of the counter-attack westwards, subsequently described 15 August as 'the worst day of my life'. In addition to the looming disaster in Normandy, that day had seen the successful landing and advance of Allied forces on the Mediterranean coast of France. To cap it all, Field Marshal von Kluge had vanished somewhere in Normandy and Hitler, shaken by the unsuccessful attempt on his life, believed he had defected. In a rage, Hitler immediately replaced him with Field Marshal Walter Model, summoned from the Russian Front. In fact von Kluge had been caught on the battlefield by Allied fighter-bombers which caused him to spend most of the day hiding in a ditch. Driving back to Germany after being relieved of his command, von Kluge committed suicide.

The great pay-off of Montgomery's deliberate pulling-in of the mass of the German armour against the British had finally arrived. Now, with Falaise almost lost, the I SS Panzer Corps there was utterly exhausted, the 85 Division virtually annihilated, and the 12 SS Panzer Division had lost all but fifteen of its tanks. None of the reinforcements promised had been able to get through. The corps seeking to hold the British at Condé, 16 miles south-west of Falaise, had nearly expended all its ammunition and Leclerc's 2 Free French were sweeping up menacingly behind them from around Ecouché, rapidly narrowing the gap which was the only German escape route. The Falaise pocket contained the mass of the German armour and guns and crack troops who had survived the prolonged fury of the fighting around Caen. Meanwhile, as Patton's armoured divisions raced onwards, another and more widely scattered pocket was forming which also faced being trapped. 'It became evident that the XX Corps was hitting nothing, so we moved it north-east of Le Mans,' noted Patton. 'The XV Corps, consisting of the 5th Armoured, 2nd French Armoured, 90th and 79th Division, could easily have entered Falaise and completely closed the gap, but we were ordered not to do this, allegedly because the British had sown the area with a large number of time bombs. [In fact, the US Ninth Air Force had dropped delayed-action bombs on the Argentan–Falaise road during the evening of 12 August, timed to explode within twelve hours.] This halt was a great mistake, as I was certain that we could have entered Falaise.'

Patton's assertion was not borne out by the testimonies of many of the men involved in this fighting. In the Forêt d'Ecouves 2 French Armoured had sustained heavy casualties, running up against determined German panzer troops dug-in and resolute in the dark depths of the forest. Gaston Eve was a corporal in a French Sherman:

'We had just seemed to keep driving on with nothing much in the way to stop us, and cheers and wine and flowers and kisses all the way. But when we reached the forest we learned what war was really all about. It was something of a shock. The leading tank was a sort of guinea pig to discover where the enemy guns were. Often it was knocked out with the first shot and the crew were killed.'

Another Free French tank soldier, Emil Fray, recalls:

'We had been going all day with hardly any fighting. Then suddenly in the middle of the forest a big battle blew up. We received a radio message telling our tank to move up front. We passed some that had already been blown up and they looked a terrible sight. Past a cross-roads the Germans had felled trees right across the road. They opened fire. They had sunk a Tiger tank level with the road with just the turret visible. I fired back again and again and it was all tremendous explosions and smoke and concussion until the sergeant in the turret gave me a big knock on the head and I realised he meant me to get out. Our tank was in flames. The two drivers had been killed. Tanks were burning everywhere.'

The Free French had bumped head-on into a formidable German blocking force hastily formed from units of the retreating 116 and 9 Panzer Divisions. Their massing had been made possible because a French thrust around the forest of Ecouves had denied the road to a petrol convoy sent to refuel the US 5 Armoured Division. They had been halted for six hours and prevented from storming Argentan before the German tanks got there. As for Patton's later assertion that he could easily have closed the Falaise gap, Omar Bradley wrote:

'Monty had never prohibited, and I had never proposed, that US forces close the gap. Although Patton might have spun a line across the narrow neck, I doubted his ability to hold it. Nineteen German divisions were now stampeding to escape. Meanwhile, with four divisions George was already blocking three principal escape routes through Alençon, Sees and Argentan. Had he stretched that line to include Falaise, the enemy could not only have broken through but might have trampled Patton's positions in the onrush. I much preferred a solid shoulder at Argentan to the possibility of a broken neck at Falaise.'

But the Germans were not yet 'stampeding to escape the trap'. They were still fighting bitterly to prevent it being closed, the bulk against the British, Canadians and Poles. Three Canadian Divisions and one from the British XII Corps were battling forward in three converging attacks within two miles of Falaise. But enemy formations could continue to escape towards the Seine and did so with all the urgency and disorder commonly associated with military disaster. Suddenly the German front was contracting on all sides, the pocket dwindling like a pricked balloon. Everywhere the Allied divisions were moving in determinedly upon them, the British, Canadians and Poles from the north and west, and the Americans and Free French from the south. The US V Corps had taken over Patton's divisions forward at Argentan on 17 August and prepared to attack north-eastwards to Trun and Chambois. All over the battlefield the men of the French Resistance, the

Maquis, swarmed into action. They sniped, rounded up bemused German stragglers, mopped up in the wake of advancing
Allied troops, and committed delaying acts of sabotage. There
were now some 100,000 Germans, the remnants of 15 battered
divisions mixed up with stragglers from around 12 more, milling
around in the swiftly shrinking pocket. Squeezed into an area
20 miles wide and 10 miles deep, they were being horrifyingly
slaughtered by an intensifying bombardment of bombers and
relentlessly rocketed and raked by the cannons and machine-
guns of fighter bombers and fighters.

The Allied artillery had closed in to lethally effective range
and was pouring thousands of shells into this tumultuous cauldron.

'Germans charred coal-black, looking like blackened tree
trunks, lay beside smoking vehicles,' remembers Duncan
Kyle. 'One didn't realise that the obscene mess was human
until it was poked at. I remember wishing that the Germans
didn't have to use so many horses. Seeing all those dead
animals on their backs, their legs pointing at God's sky like
accusing fingers, their bellies bloated, some ripped open . . .
That really bothered me. The road to Falaise was nauseating.
I felt like puking many times, what butchery! The air force
did its job well.'

Only two escape routes remained, narrow roads leading
through Chambois and St Lambert, both under heavy fire. On
16 August the Canadian 2 Division burst into Falaise from the
west. General Crerar named Trun, 16 miles south-east of
Falaise, as the immediate Canadian objective and Lisieux, 25
miles north-east, as the objective of the British I Corps. Montgomery had informed Crerar he believed the Panzer divisions
still west of Argentan would try to break out between there and
Falaise and would then flee north-eastwards. Trun, standing
squarely in the centre of the existing gap, the junction of several
roads, was thus vitally important. All that survived of the
German Seventh Army along with nearly half the Fifth Panzer
Army had still not passed through.

On 19 August a group comprising 14 Sherman tanks of the

South Alberta Regiment, and one understrength company of the Canadian Argyll and Sutherland Highlanders totalling no more than 125 officers and men, seized the village of St Lambert-sur-Dives in the midst of the main stream of German retreat. But although they stubbornly split that stream they could not stem it. And so it was with other British, Canadian and Polish formations that sought to plug the gap. None was individually strong enough to prevent powerful panzer groups punching through and to halt the headlong flow. Meanwhile a still formidable remnant of the II SS Panzer Corps concentrated beyond the Falaise gap to break it open from the east if closed. As the battle reached its tumultuous climax, resolute soldiers of the Fifth Panzer Army facing northwards to Falaise, and of Eberbach's armoured group facing south to Argentan, kept the gap open.

The heroic Canadians in St Lambert continued to shatter enemy formations seeking escape, despite themselves sustaining casualties amounting to one third of their numbers, increased by reinforcements from the Canadian Argylls and Lincoln and Welland Regiment. Major D. Currie, in command of this heroic little force, even called down the fire of the British and Canadian guns upon the village to increase the havoc. Somehow the bridge across the Dives there remained intact to provide escape for the fleeing Germans. But such was the concentration of fire on its approaches and surrounds that the river was almost choked with the bodies of men and horses and wrecked enemy armour, vehicles and guns. The streets ran with the blood of the German soldiers and horses, pulped by the tracks of grinding panzers and jolting lorries.

The Allied guns and aircraft subjected the retreating enemy to a bombardment possibly unparalleled in the history of warfare. Although the proximity of Allied troops to the desperate Germans was such that the bombers could attack targets no nearer than Vimoutiers, 19 miles east of Falaise and 10 miles north-east of Trun, the fighters performed a frightful execution. They scoured the countryside to devastate fleeing enemy transport beyond Vimoutiers and near Lisieux and to sink troop transport barges on the Seine.

Montgomery ordered the Canadians to capture Trun as quickly as possible while Bradley's First Army attacked north-eastwards. This should effectively trap the German Seventh Army. The German front line ran southwards from Coubourg on the Channel coast 24 kilometres north-east of Caen, then bulged eastwards across the Dives where the British I Corps and Canadian II Corps had respectively secured bridge-heads at St Pierre-sur-Dives and near Jort. From there it ran south-west to the environs of Falaise. Westwards from there to Condé the Fifth Panzer Army confronted the Canadian First and British Second Armies while along a line southwards from Condé towards Domfront the battered German Seventh Army faced the British and then the American First Army along their southern flank eastwards to the River Rouvre beyond Briouze. From the river eastwards this flank was then defended by Panzer Group Eberbach. The tearaway thrusts Patton's armoured columns had already made far beyond to Chartres and Orléans had given cause for Montgomery to cancel an airborne operation planned between the Seine and the Loire. The whereabouts of some of these thrusts were not even known by Patton.

Inevitably in such a confused and confusing battlefield there were mistakes by the Allied air forces.

'On August 16 we moved to Egbed-Cremesnil. The dust was so thick it was impossible to see more than a few yards,' remembers Colin Thomson. 'We moved over the bridge at St Pierre-sur-Dives to work up the line of the river. The village was [full] of burnt out vehicles. I learned later that some of our Lancasters bombed a mixture of 51st Highland Division and the Polish Division by mistake . . . From St Pierre-sur-Dives we slogged on through Linerot where one of our sergeants was [attacked] by a horde of drunken SS with swords! The platoon of the Queen's with us rebuffed the assault after a stiff fight.'

16 The Closing of the Gap

Model, on his first day as C-in-C West, ordered Hauser to withdraw all that remained of his army to a new line along the Dives. He first had to launch the II SS Panzer Corps in a desperate counter-attack from the east against the Canadians around Morteau and the Poles who were also battering forward to Trun. The Polish 1 Armoured Division, suddenly switched from attacking towards Falaise to make a dramatic thrust north-eastwards, sent Cromwells to seize a crossing over the Dives at Jort. Nine surviving tanks churned across a muddy ford to attack the bridge defences in the rear and the Germans withdrew from Jort suffering severe casualties under heavy artillery fire. Soon more Polish armour and infantry arrived and consolidated. Nevertheless, the gap was still open, even if a death trap for those using it. Columns of German transport seeking to escape by daylight along the Chambois–Vimoutiers road were devastated by British and American aircraft. This road, with its feeder roads on each side, looked like a fiery herringbone to the Allied pilots for everywhere German tanks, troop carriers, gun tractors and supply vehicles were jammed nose to tail burning, exploding, littered with dead and dying men.

Although the crack Waffen SS still fought bitterly and to the death to hold open the narrow corridor south of Falaise, most Germans were now only concerned with escaping. Through the one escape gap between Trun and Chambois were streaming, under conditions of mounting panic, the remnants of the German armoured divisions and battle groups which had for so long been fighting the British and Canadians around Caen. In addition, there were the new formations which had belatedly, hopelessly, thrust westwards. German tanks, self-propelled

guns, armoured troop-carriers, artillery drawn by vehicles or by
horses, and disorganised infantry soldiers by the thousands, in
or on vehicles, sprawled across tanks, slumped in lumbering
farm carts, pedalling bicycles or trudging wearily, were all in
the flood of defeated enemy seeking escape. The Allied artillery
and aircraft continued to attack the retreating enemy, and inflicted very great casualties not only on the Germans but also
upon French civilians attempting to escape from the wholesale
slaughter in which they were caught up. At night, as the
merciless bombardment continued, the sky was lit up with
the flames of burning tanks, vehicles and villages and the continuous eruption of shells and bombs. Charles Best, Battery
Sergeant Major of the 67 Anti-Tank Battery, saw the results:

'Along the Vire–Falaise road I came to a stretch for two
miles choc-a-bloc with German dead bodies and vehicles,
even horse gun teams. It was the most terrifying sight, I had
seen—a massacre! The British rocket-firing Typhoons had
caught them in close formation. There must have been a
major traffic jam when they struck.'

Frederic Wilkinson recalls:

'The scene was terrible—overturned tanks, heavy armoured
vehicles blasted out of recognition, upturned guns, even
horse drawn vehicles, all blown up. The stench of death from
all the decomposing bodies lying about was indescribable. I
had the smell on my uniform for weeks.'

As the British Second Army pressed forward determinedly
they were challenged by German rearguards behind extensive
minefields along the line of the Rouvre. Keeping pace, and in
touch with the British, the American First Army attacked towards Briouze. The Germans had now retreated between 4 and
8 miles although the rearmost divisions still had up to 15 miles
to cover before they would be within escaping distance of the
gap. Their more fortunate comrades not so deeply committed
had been moving out as fast as they could. Montgomery had

K

ordered that the Canadian 4 and Polish 1 Armoured Divisions should capture Trun and then Chambois quickly and regardless of cost, no simple task in the broken hilly country. The I SS Panzer Corps, recently reinforced by the 21 Panzers, was bitterly contesting the Canadian and Polish advance. Canadian tanks had been held three miles north of Trun and a mile short of the Vimoutiers road. The foremost Polish tanks had been halted by a formidable screen of anti-tank guns short of that vital road.

The American First Army, pressing northwards on the pocket, had yet to open its assault on Chambois. A Polish armoured column on the left wing of the Canadian attack travelled by night to reach Champeaux on the Trun–Vimoutiers road. As the leading tanks entered the village a man in pyjamas emerged from a house, took one look and shouted: 'Feindliche Panzer!' A number of pyjama-clad figures dashed out and disappeared pursued by machine-gun fire. In the house the eager Poles found two generals' uniforms. It was the HQ of the II Panzer SS Corps! A search revealed a stack of suitcases filled with loot, including Parisian gowns, furs, ladies' underwear, jewellery and silverware. A company of German infantry marching to investigate was mown down by the waiting Shermans. The Polish tank column—the Polish 2 Armoured Regiment commanded by Colonel Stanislaw Koszutski—had in fact arrived in Champeaux both unintentionally and fortuitously. They had intended to enter Chambois and had engaged a French guide to lead them. He however had proved false and deliberately led them into Champeaux, the very headquarters of the German command that even then was planning a massive panzer counter-attack from the east to rescue the force trapped in the Falaise pocket. The totally unexpected arrival of Koszutski's tanks in Champeaux threw the Germans into such confusion that their counter-attack was delayed for forty-eight hours. This not only undoubtedly saved the exposed Polish division from annihilation but also allowed time for the British and Canadians to bring sufficient force forward to meet the counter-attack.

Trun was vital to the enemy, being the last gateway to the

existing escape routes. The Canadian 4 Armoured Division was ordered to seize the dominating heights while the town itself was captured by the Poles. Well hidden German anti-tank guns exacted a steady toll as the Canadian tanks advanced cross-country but that night the Lake Superior Regiment and Grenadiers fought into Trun. The tanks of the Foot Guards next occupied Point 118 near Louvières-en-Auge, discovering a Polish motor battalion already there. Here they dominated the Falaise–Trun and Trun–Vimoutiers roads, of which fact the enemy indicated their awareness by subjecting the Canadians and Poles to heavy bombardment. Moving by night to a new position on the heights, the Foot Guards were joined by the Lake Superior Regiment. From there they moved to an even steeper hill which gave them a magnificent view over the valley to Trun and Chambois and further across the great Normandy plain.

Early next day the Polish tanks deployed across the River Dives began to explode, shelled by an SS Division attempting to escape along the valley. Soon the sky was filled with rocket-firing Typhoons, and black smoke rolled from burning German tanks, self-propelled guns and supply vehicles, and the enemy infantry was mown down in swathes by Canadian and Polish machine-guns.

The I SS Panzer Corps fought back with a fury born of desperation. Canadian armoured spearheads were halted outside St Lambert-sur-Dives and Polish tanks were checked in the hilly terrain around Coudehard. Both forces were still some three miles from Chambois, as were the Americans attacking from the south. The gap was still six miles wide. But what had not been achieved by the often desperate bravery of the attacking British, Canadians, Poles, French and Americans was almost achieved by the Second Tactical Air Force. After flying close on 1,500 sorties the Second Tactical Air Force alone could claim 90 tanks and 1,100 vehicles destroyed, a further 100 tanks and 1,500 vehicles damaged, and an incalculable number of German soldiers killed.

Through most of 19 August the Canadian 4 Armoured Division, with infantry reinforcements, endeavoured to batter through to St Lambert, where Currie and his brave men were still taking a hideous toll of the Germans streaming past them on both sides. The Canadian artillery and machine-guns had the escape avenues closely covered and were slaughtering the retreating enemy. Meanwhile Currie's men, under constant assault, beat off each and every attack.

The Poles, equally isolated amidst a constant stream of retreating enemy, fought off repeated attacks. 'The Germans had been encircled as in a bottle, and you were the cork in that bottle,' Montgomery was to tell the Poles admiringly. The Polish 1 Armoured, so exhausted from the ceaseless action that men fell instantly asleep the moment they stopped, even when driving tanks, moved up on to Hill 262 on 19 August. It was the summit of a bare massif so steep that the soldiers had wondered whether they were approaching Switzerland. It was on the only remaining escape routes open to the Germans, whether they took the main Chambois–Trun road or tried to filter away through lanes and tracks. Along the last ridge the Poles took up positions and at once found targets. Immediately below them came a closely packed convoy of Germans made up of Panthers and other tanks, tractor-towed guns, lorry-borne infantry, horse-drawn guns and waggons loaded with soldiers, armoured cars and ancient civilian cars, anything on wheels which would carry the retreating enemy.

All together the long line of Polish tanks opened fire with guns and machine guns. Flames and smoke instantly enveloped the crawling procession. Soldiers toppled and leapt from tanks, cars and carts. The German tanks were fatally trapped among the horse-drawn carts. They could not aim their guns at the Poles above them, and were at the mercy of the Polish 17-pound anti-tank guns. The only Germans to escape were those who stumbled out waving white rags or crawled out wounded. Then a Polish infantry battalion arrived to reinforce the tanks. Again and again they fired upon formations of Germans trying to pass the hilltop fortress. More and more surrendered, though some were deliberately shot down by their own tanks. The Germans realised that they must smash through this Polish position or accept that one of their last escape routes was closed. German artillery subjected the bare hilltop to a mounting bombardment. The guns of the Polish tanks continued to fire upon enemy columns. The tired Polish gunners were struck by the slowness with which the grey-uniformed soldiers tried to walk out of range. Here was a greater weariness even than theirs. Formations of 21 Panzers and SS divisions desperately tried to blast a way through. Polish tanks went up in flames as the 88mm guns of Panther tanks hit them, but the Poles struck back with the fury of men with a bitter score to settle. German shells fell among the hundreds of prisoners cowering in close-packed groups among the Poles. At point-blank range the cleverly camouflaged Polish 17-pounders destroyed charging panzers, including Panthers and Tigers. Meanwhile artillery observers, one from a Canadian medium regiment, brought down the fire of their batteries all around the Polish hilltop fortress upon the attackers.

The final concerted assault was made early on 21 August when a company of German infantry, shouting madly, desperately charged up the steepest slope. They were mown down. Soon the enemy artillery and mortar fire dwindled, their machine-guns fell silent, and no more panzers came. The Poles had held their hilltop fortress that blocked the last but one possible escape route. Then, short of fuel, they moved on to Chambois, a once pretty little Normandy town set among orchards and folds of hills. The Trun–Chambois road seemed totally empty. Could the enemy have left? But reconnaissance revealed Chambois packed with Germans. Soon Allied fighter-bombers attacked them and the street billowed smoke from burning tanks, vehicles and houses. A squadron of Polish Cromwells thrust in to the town and waited for reinforcement by the 10 Dragoon Regiment, whose foremost squadron burst through a German artillery barrage to flank the only remaining escape road.

Unable to get through streets jammed with burned-out panzers, Second Lieut Karcz pushed on through gardens towards the River Dives. Suddenly he saw the round helmets of probably a whole battalion of infantry advancing. A burst of Polish machine-gun fire caused them to fling themselves to the ground, and white handkerchiefs waved. Congratulating himself on taking a whole battalion prisoner, Karcz stepped out. The nearest man got up and ran forward, arms held out in greeting rather than surrender. His helmet was not a normal German helmet. Instead of German field boots he wore rubber-soled boots and tight gaiters. The man was grinning broadly. He was an American! The Polish 1 Armoured Division and the American First Army had met! Soon Leclerc's Free French also fought in from the south. The trap had been snapped shut. Unfortunately it was soon made less effective because Leclerc had, not unnaturally, become obsessed with being first into Paris. He kept urging Bradley to let him make a dash for Paris, until Bradley let his division go.

The Canadian 4 Armoured Division moved north-east to Vimoutiers, still sustaining cruel casualties from 88mm guns. They were to block a reported break-out attempt by a large German armoured column which soon appeared, firing furiously. But the Canadians were dug-down in good defensive positions. Their fire-power was formidable and soon German tanks were aflame and close-packed infantry were shot down. There was no hope for them. A crowd of wild-eyed battle-stained German soldiers stumbled forward in surrender and, although most were crack SS troops, many claimed they were Poles or Czechs. Although there were Polish and Czech soldiers pressed into service by the Germans, many German soldiers were eager to deny their nationality now their once victorious armies were finally being called to account.

The Falaise gap was finally closed on 21 August when a brigade of the Canadian 4 Armoured Division fought through to the Poles at Coudehard and the Canadian 3 and 4 Divisions penetrated to St Lambert and thence to Chambois. The British 53 Division meanwhile advanced to join the Canadians near Trun. That day saw the last attempt, by II SS Panzer Corps, to force the trap from outside. They counter-attacked the Poles on their ridge and for a time had them cut off, so that they had to be supplied from the air. But the Poles did not yield and the Canadians joined in to halt this attack. Then Allied aircraft found the SS Panzers, destroyed most of their fuel and attacked their armoured vehicles and support lorries. They joined the general retreat.

All that remained of Hauser's armour disintegrated beneath bombardment at the approaches to Trun and Chambois, caught in the devastation of wrecked transport already there. The only way out was over the open fields in the face of the terrible fire of the concentrated Allied artillery, mortars, machine-guns and aircraft. Inevitably the slaughter was dreadful as German soldiers, now fleeing in utter terror, sought to escape on foot. They were led by the survivors of the II Parachute Corps and Panzer Group Eberbach. Among those who did manage to escape were Generals Hauser, Eugen Meindl, commander of the II Parachute Corps, and Kurt Meyer. Hauser, badly wounded, was taken out by a group of panzers; Meindl got through with a paratroop bodyguard; Meyer, later sentenced to death for the execution of Canadian prisoners (a sentence which was commuted) was actually led out by a French civilian.

In the last pocket 344 tanks, self-propelled guns and other armoured vehicles, 2,447 lorries and cars and 252 towed guns were later counted. It was also estimated 8,000 horses had been killed there. Eisenhower said afterwards that: 'The battlefield at Falaise was unquestionably one of the greatest killing grounds of any of the war areas. Roads, highways and fields were so choked with destroyed equipment and with dead men and animals that passage through the area was extremely difficult. Forty-eight hours after the closing of the gap, I was conducted through it on foot to encounter scenes that could be described only by Dante.'

In addition to the slaughter of some 10,000 Germans during the six days when they tried to escape through the gap, 50,000 prisoners were taken. Of the 20–50,000 who escaped, many were killed before they reached the Seine. Thousands more, cut off elsewhere, also surrendered. Eight divisions of infantry and two panzer divisions were captured almost complete. The armies to which Hitler had entrusted the destruction of the Allies in the West had been utterly routed. Their total casualties in Normandy were over 450,000 (240,000 killed and wounded and 210,000 prisoners), 1,500 tanks, 3,500 guns and 20,000 vehicles. Excluding the enemy garrisons trapped in the Brittany ports and Channel Islands, a total of 43 German divisions had been destroyed or rendered barely operational. Against this the Allies lost 209,672 men of whom 36,976 were killed. The Germans had set out on a headlong flight from which they were not to recover until behind the German frontier 325 miles east.

General George Smith Patton Jnr, suddenly the most popular American general by virtue of his army's spectacular drive around the southern flank of the Normandy battlefield, was leading his tearaway armoured columns flat out—for the German frontier, virtually unopposed.

Index

Note : The general index is preceded by a list of the military formations involved in the battle.